W9-AOC-000

FINAL REPORT

Mennonite International Study Project

NANCY HEISEY AND PAUL LONGACRE

Eastern Mennonite Board of Missions and Charities
Franconia Mennonite Conference Mission Commission
Mennonite Board of Missions
Mennonite Central Committee
Virginia Mennonite Board of Missions

1990

Sponsored by the following agencies:

Eastern Mennonite Board of Missions and Charities
P.O. Box 128, Salunga, PA 17538-0628

Franconia Mennonite Conference Mission Commission
Box 116, Souderton, PA 18964

Mennonite Board of Missions
Box 370, Elkhart, IN 46515-0370

Mennonite Central Committee
Box 500, Akron, PA 17501-0500

Virginia Mennonite Board of Missions
901 Parkwood Drive, Harrisonburg, VA 22801

ISBN 1-877736-04-X

Printed in the United States of America

Outline

Preface

We wish to make a few comments at the beginning of this more formally printed edition of our final report. Six months after the report was written, we have met with each of the sponsoring agencies to discuss the report. In addition, a meeting of the administrators of the sponsoring agencies has been held to discuss their responses to the report. We have also had many significant comments from individuals who read it.

These six months have been valuable for us to reflect on our experience and our effort to encapsulate it in writing. We continue to feel that the report accurately reflects what we heard and felt in our two years of travel and conversations. While there might be minor restatements or more detailed explanations at a few places, on the whole the report stands, except for one glaring omission--a call to prayer.

Repeatedly when we asked overseas church people what they would like of the North American church they said: "Pray for us." We felt that this statement expressed their understanding of the most important way as well as at times the only way we in North America can be involved with sisters and brothers around the world. This plea for prayer is a recognition of our dependence upon the head of the Church, Jesus Christ our Lord, and of our unity with one another as members of the church around the world.

--Nancy Heisey and Paul Longacre

Christianity will divide in North America--
and there are already signs of that beginning to
take place--not on inerrancy of Scripture and not
on other forms of doctrine that we debate and
discuss. It will divide on whether the church of
Jesus is that which seeks controlling power--to
rule, to dictate, to mandate, to legislate--or the
church that takes the way of servanthood, which
is the crest of history in Christ's future plan.

--Richard Detweiler

Note of thanks

To begin we must say thank you. If our list of acknowledgements were complete, it would be too long for this paper. Since it is not, we may fail by missing someone in whose debt we are. Nevertheless we say simply, thank you:

-- to all of our hosts, who cooked for and served us, prepared our beds, offered endless cups of tea and coffee, accompanied us on foot, in buses and jeepneys, picked us up and dropped us off, talked freely with us, welcomed us and bade us farewell as sister and brother;

-- to the more than 1400 people who took our questions seriously and opened their hearts to us in response;

-- to those who helped us organize our itineraries and schedules, who wrote us letters, sent us telexes, rearranged and fitted things in, hauled us around, translated for us, gave us cash advances and made sure the bills were paid;

-- to the administrators and members of our reference group who read our reports, asked questions, followed our travels with interest, and are left with figuring out what to make of all this;

-- to our families and our church family for letters, prayers, taking care of things in our absences, seeing us off and meeting us over and over;

-- to the children who sat on our laps, went for walks with us, and asked us for stories. They reminded us of both the nature of the kingdom of God and the importance of the future of the church in mission.

Introduction

We the writers began this two-year study with many apprehensions about what Christians around the world would want to say to North Americans committed to mission at the end of the twentieth century. As we complete the work, we admit to being surprised and encouraged by the messages we received from sisters and brothers. Through their voices we heard a new call for North American Christians to take the way of servanthood. In following that way, we believe there are challenges and opportunities ahead which we can take up with joy.

We are called:

-- to encourage and support those in other places as they proclaim the gospel,

-- to join in the struggle in many places for justice, peace and the integrity of creation,

-- to work together with others around the world in service to those in need.

We are challenged:

-- to call, train and send the kind of people our sisters and brothers in other places need to help them in their task, and to receive those they send to us,

-- to contribute freely and more of our financial wealth toward new ways of carrying out the mission task,

-- to give up a measure of decision-making control about the use of our personnel and financial resources,

-- to begin developing structures which give more voice and power to churches with whom we work on mission tasks in other places.

We are offered the opportunity:

-- in a time of economic crisis and disintegration, to find greater and more creative ways of sharing resources,

-- in a time of political conflict, to build deeper commitment to the church as a worldwide body of Christ, a community whose life and witness challenge the powers that be,

-- in a time of spiritual poverty in our own society, to learn from the wealth of spiritual resources in the churches in many other places,

-- in a time of religious and ideological struggle, to understand more fully the common faith of all followers of Jesus, a faith found in many forms but guided by one Spirit.

The text of this report suggests in more detail how the writers understand these gifts, challenges and calls.

I. Background to the Mennonite International Study Project

A. Expanded mission interest in the churches

According to the 1986 MARC Handbook, "the North American mission community has . . . taken aim on 2000 A.D." Examples include:

-- "Southern Baptists talk about presenting the gospel to every person in the world by the century's end."

-- "United Methodists are challenged to double church membership in the U.S. by the year 2000."

-- "Frontiers, Inc. aims to recruit 200 teams, ten persons a team, for 'planting the church among 200 Muslim people groups by the year 2000.' "

-- "The 'frontier missions' movement, associated with Ralph Winter and the U.S. Center for World Mission, calls for a 'church for every people by the year 2000' " (MARC 1986:35).

Meetings on mission issues abound. In 1987 a group of 100 people gathered in Connecticut, U.S., to discuss Catholic and Protestant mission. In February 1989, a gathering in Stuttgart, West Germany, brought together representatives of the Lausanne Committee for World Evangelization (LCWE), the World Council of Churches and the World Evangelical Fellowship to discuss evangelism in the world context. In May 1989, the Commission on World Mission and Evangelism of the WCC held the tenth international mission conference since 1910, with the theme: "Your Will Be Done: Mission in Christ's Way." In July 1989, LCWE held Lausanne II in Manila, Philippines, with the theme "Proclaim Christ Until He Comes--Calling the Whole Church to take the Whole Gospel to the Whole World."

Statistician David Barrett, editor of the *World Christian Encyclopedia*, is the dean of a growing school of people seeking to quantify and categorize worldwide church growth. In a recent article, Barrett lists 19

Christian global megatrends, including: rise of 56 global ministry networks with 42 million computers, mushrooming of literature on evangelization (10,000 items a year), proliferation of 400 conferences on evangelization a year, 50 new global plans for world evangelization a year and 2,500 evangelistic mass campaigns a year (Barrett 1989:29).

B. The Mennonite Church vision

It is within this end-of-the-millennium environment that the Mennonite Church in 1985 took a look at its own goals for mission and evangelism for the following decade. Included among those goals, which have come to be known as Vision 95, was the goal "to increase the number of workers supported in mission beyond North America from about 500 to more than 1,000." As Mennonite mission administrators discussed how to implement this particular goal, they agreed that the mood of the North American churches which had expressed it was one of expectation, of wanting to be challenged, of being ready to grow and expand. They decided that each agency would quickly initiate consultation with their overseas partner churches to collect ideas and advice which would direct further planning.

Late in 1986 a proposal was circulated among five Mennonite Church mission boards--Eastern Mennonite Board of Missions, Franconia Conference Mission Commission, Mennonite Board of Missions, Rosedale Mennonite Missions and Virginia Mennonite Mission Board--and the Mennonite Central Committee, suggesting an additional process to obtain counsel from Christians in other parts of the world. It suggested providing a staff person to study "the world situation generally and countries or regions specifically with a view to discovering fresh approaches and opportunities for Christian ministry," and to engage "in dialogue with counterparts in other countries representing a variety of perspectives a) with view to program that responds more fully to the requirements in a particular situation in light of discernable trends and prospects; b) in order to open up possibilities for multi-lateral relationships in program (rather than maintaining the present unilateral approach)."

In March 1987 representatives of the five boards which had agreed to participate in such a project (not including Rosedale) met with Paul Longacre and Nancy Heisey and drafted the following statement of the assignment the agencies were proposing to the couple: "To arrange settings where we can listen to Christians in other countries and cultures communicate their vision for evangelism, outreach, and Christian service in order to discover what role North American Christians should play in the worldwide community of faith, and bring back suggestions of creative methods and models through which we can participate with them in extending God's rule in the world." The group concluded that for the effort to be effective, it would be essential to lis-

2

ten to the national churches, to discover our role, and identify specific, practical steps.

C. Carrying out
the study project

Having accepted the assignment by these five agencies to arrange for the conversations called for in the statement, the writers laid out a work plan. Instructions were that the

> *We northerners always pick up a problem and turn it around, away from ourselves. Shouldn't your listening settings be in North America? --European church service agency administrator*

project run for two years with half-time travel internationally. The writers chose the title "Mennonite International Study Project" for the work, hoping to identify what we were doing (studying) and who we were working for (Mennonites) but to avoid preconceived ideas among those we would be meeting. A project proposal together with a budget was prepared and used as the basis for our planning (Appendix 1).

The writers arranged to make four three-month trips, one each to Europe, Asia, Latin America and Africa. We included brief stops in the Middle East on our Europe and Asia trips. We visited 45 countries with an average length of stay in a country of 8.5 days. Contacts were arranged for us by church leaders, North American Mennonite workers assigned in certain countries, and through direct correspondence which we initiated with people whose names had been suggested to us.

The work procedure was to conduct interviews with individuals or small groups in every place visited. Rather than using an extensive questionnaire, we pursued open-ended discussions based on four questions which were circulated to our informants ahead of time as often as feasible (Appendix 2). We met approximately 1450 people in more than 460 interview sessions. These informants represented 27 different Chris-

> *I am glad you came to visit. No one has ever asked me questions like that before. --Tanzanian Mennonite businessman*

tian denominations and a variety of interchurch groups. (All Mennonites and Brethren in Christ, all Presbyterian groups, all Pentecostal groups, and so on, were included in the count as one denomination.) In a few instances we had the privilege of interviewing persons of other faiths who had some working relationship or history with Mennonites. We joined in worship services of all kinds and lengths whenever possible, and attempted to pick up ideas during informal social contacts as well as in scheduled interviews. Everywhere we were graciously received and hosted, and often we were thanked for coming.

After each trip we prepared a country-by-country summary of what we had heard. These reports were sent back to as many of our infor-

3

mants as possible, as well as to administrators of the sponsoring agencies and members of a reference group which the agencies had appointed for us. We met with the administrators and reference group after each trip to discuss the issues raised and receive further guidance.

> We did not get enough information about your visit ahead of time to plan. If there is another chance, we will come in greater numbers to discuss these issues with you. --Indian Mennonite pastor

The writers realized in the process of carrying out the project that urgent questions about mission and the yearning to discern the future of the church are present throughout the churches around the world. We also realized that often what people had to say to us was not new. Occasionally we heard a very striking or unexpected assessment of a situation. But most of the messages we received had a very familiar ring to them. Assuming the limitations of our own hearing, we became convinced that brothers and sisters worldwide as well as many North American mission and service workers have been doing the job of communicating how Christians elsewhere view the world and the church's task in it. Our privilege was to receive the reinforcement of hearing the same messages repeated in different places, from people in a variety of unique circumstances. The question for North Americans, as it has been, is: "What are we going to do about what we know?"

While the sense of common themes was very strong, we also heard a great many different things. Situations varied from region to region and country to country. Different church groups have had different histories with their related mission bodies and have accepted different theological assumptions. Some informants felt free to speak while others were very cautious. The writers' ability to hear across barriers of language, cultural differences and fatigue, was limited. Informants' past experiences with North Americans affected how they shaped their messages to us.

Thus it is unrealistic to say in a report such as this that we are presenting the voice of Christians around the world. What the writers have done is to attempt to pick out themes which were repeated and ideas about which there was large consensus. The writers are also expressing our own opinions in many cases, opinions which we hope are largely shaped by the conversations we have had and our reflections on them. The intention of this report, as with every other part of the MISP process, is to create a forum for further discussion. While this represents the project's final statement, we hope that it is only the beginning of some new conversations.

II. The Bible and Mission

A. Mennonite mission statements

Christians around the world emphasize the importance of the Bible, and most Christian groups who describe their call to mission use the Bible to explain what they are doing and why they are doing it.

Mennonites think of ourselves as biblical people. In the early stages of this study project, one of the clearest critiques of the project's terms was that they did not include a clear statement of the biblical understandings about the church in mission. The writers agreed with our critics, after some discussion, that the project did not have as a central task to do background biblical study which had already been done in Mennonite missiological circles. Examples of such documents include the 1980 Eastern Mennonite Board Statement "Pilgrimage in Mission," the 1978 Mennonite Board of Missions statement "A Theology of Mission in Outline," and the 1988 *Mission Focus* pamphlet "God's New Economy: Interdependence and Mission."

In 1988 14 member agencies of the Council of International Ministries--the inter-Mennonite and Brethren in Christ mission consultative body--brought together short statements outlining their theologies of mission and their missiological stances. Eight of these statements referred to the Great Commission (Matt. 28:18-20) as a foundational understanding for their work. Four referred to the kingdom of God, two stated that their understandings were founded on the entire Bible, two listed a variety of Old and New Testament passages, one referred to the incarnation and one to the eschatological vision of making all things new.

The strong emphasis on the Great Commission in these statements was further bolstered by the many references to those who are the focus of the sending out--"all peoples," "all nations," "people groups," or "unreached peoples" (the latter two terms following current attempts in some missiological circles to give new understanding to the translation of Matthew 28's *panta ta ethne*). While several statements referred to economic and political realities, only two referred specifically to a call to be among the "poor" or "the needy," indicating that the emphasis of other missiological circles on "the preferential option for the poor" is less influential on Mennonite thinking.

B. Talking about the Great Commission

> *And Jesus came and said to them, "All authority in heaven and on earth has been given to me. Go therefore and make disciples of all nations, baptizing them in the name of the Father and of the Son and of the Holy Spirit, teaching them to observe all that I have commanded you; and lo, I am with you always, to the close of the Age" (Matthew 28:18-20).*

The emphasis on the Great Commission is normal for mission and service agencies coming from the Anabaptist tradition. As historian Franklin Littell writes:

> *No words of the Master were given more serious attention by his Anabaptist followers than his final command . . . The proof text appears repeatedly in Anabaptist sermons and apologetic writings. The large body of court testimonies and confessions of faith recently made available indicate its central significance, and the various series of questions prepared by the authorities for use in court indicate that they expected it to be of prime importance. Our faith stands on nothing other than the command of Christ (Matthew 28, Mark 16). For Christ didn't say to his disciples: "Go forth and celebrate the Mass, but go forth and preach the Gospel" (Littell in Shenk 1984:18, 19).*

We must at the same time recognize that this text has been the foundation for a great deal of western/northern mission effort whose painful results have often given the word "mission" a negative connotation. Dutch missiologist Johannes Blauw discussed the reasons for this reality. "Mission was formerly based a little too one-sidedly and (even) almost exclusively on this 'great commission.' But the fault lay not in the fact that mission was based on *this* declaration, but in the fact that Matthew 28:18-20 was isolated from the whole of the biblical witness" (Blauw 1962:85, 86). "The emphasis in the whole New Testament is always on the 'going,' but . . . this term indicates the crossing of the boundary between Israel and the Gentiles rather than geographical boundaries . . . " (Blauw 1962:111). In contrast to this biblical understanding, Blauw points out that the

> *We need to relate the whole of the biblical canon to the whole of mission. A narrow interpretation of the Macedonian call limits the Spirit to working only in Macedonia, not in Turkey, too. --British Bible professor*

modern emphasis has been to see the "uttermost parts of the earth" as faraway places. "The ends of the earth" terminology must be "purged of its non-biblical 'western' significance" if the Matthew 28 passage is to be correctly understood, he asserts (Blauw 1962:112).

In a more recent pamphlet, Lesslie Newbigin discusses mission from the basis of four New Testament texts. In reference to the Matthew 28 passage, he notes that it was never used as the basis for mission until the time of William Carey--the period now known as the Great Century of Mission. (It might be observed that the Anabaptist use of the passage described above does seem to represent a more immediate, personal and nongeographical interpretation.) Writes Newbigin:

> *There are, I think, reasons why Matthew 28:18-20 has had such a dominant, almost exclusive role in Protestant thinking about missions in the past two hundred years. Taken in isolation . . . it could seem to validate a sort of triumphalist style of mission that accorded all too easily with the political and economic expansion of the European powers during this period, an expansion with which missions were (inevitably) so much connected (Newbigin 1987:32).*

C. The gospel call to mission

Newbigin places his discussion of the Matthew 28 passage in the framework of three other New Testament passages which are found below, and to which we add one more.

Most Americans think Matthew 28 says: "Only Americans are to go into all the world and preach the gospel." Most Americans think the missionary task is to make disciples for America. -- missionary in Spain

> *Now after John was arrested, Jesus came into Galilee, preaching the gospel of God, and saying, "The time is fulfilled, and the kingdom of God is at hand; repent, and believe in the gospel." And passing along by the Sea of Galilee, he saw Simon and Andrew the brother of Simon casting a net in the sea; for they were fishermen. And Jesus said to them, "Follow me and I will make you become fishers of men." And immediately they left their nets and followed him (Mark 1:14-18).*

> *So when they had come together, they asked him, "Lord, will you at this time restore the kingdom to Israel?" He said to them, "It is not for you to know times or seasons which the Father has fixed by his own authority. But you shall receive power when the Holy Spirit has come upon you; and you shall be my witnesses in Jerusalem and in all Judea and Samaria and to the end of the earth" (Acts 1:6-8).*

> *On the evening of that day, the first day of the week, the doors being shut where the disciples were, for fear of the Jews, Jesus came*

and stood among them and said to them, "Peace be with you." When he had said this he showed them his hands and his side. Then the disciples were glad when they saw the Lord. Jesus said to them again, "Peace be with you. As the Father has sent me, even so I send you." And when he had said this, he breathed on them, and said to them, "Receive the Holy Spirit" (John 20:19-22).

And he came to Nazareth, where he had been brought up; and he went to the synagogue, as his custom was, on the Sabbath day. And he stood up to read; and there was given to him the book of the prophet Isaiah. He opened the book and found the place where it was written, "The Spirit of the Lord is upon me, because he has anointed me to preach good news to the poor. He has sent me to proclaim release to the captives and recovering of sight to the blind, to set at liberty those who are oppressed, to proclaim the acceptable year of the Lord." And he closed the book, and gave it back to the attendant, and sat down; and the eyes of all in the synagogue were fixed on him. And he began to say to them, "Today this scripture has been fulfilled in your hearing" (Luke 4:16-21).

It is tempting to simply quote from Newbigin in his exposition of the Mark, Acts, and John passages, but his comments must be read for themselves in their entirety. Rather, we simply underline here the central themes they lift up. 1) The call to follow Jesus is given in the context of the proclamation of the good news of the kingdom of God. 2) The kingdom of God has been demonstrated in Jesus, and manifests itself in what is good news for those who suffer and are oppressed. 3) The final, complete establishment of the kingdom of God is God's work in God's time; the power of the Holy Spirit moves humans to live as witnesses to Jesus Christ in the present. 4) Jesus sends out his followers as God sent him, a model known as the incarnation. 5) The model of the incarnation is one which leads people into/through suffering.

Each of these passages point backward and forward to others in the Old and New Testament, making clear that to understand what the Bible says about mission requires a broad reading. At the same time, each of these passages are so much at the center of the writers' understanding of call that we believe they must be held together in trying to define what Mennonite Christians are doing in mission. "There is no other church than the church sent into the world," writes Blauw (1962:121). To the degree that the church both understands that truth in the light of Matthew 28 and allows the other commissions to define the nature of that sending, we will be on the path to the faithfulness in mission.

III. Sent into the world as servants

A. Mission

One of the big problems in trying to discuss mission is the matter of language. There are many words which seem essential to the process of communication about mission, but their meanings have been blurred by the process of history and the many conflicts that have gone on among Christians about who is doing what in the right or wrong ways. In section III the writers offer definitions of mission and service, and

> *In the Bible neither "evangelism" nor "mission" is mentioned; but "evangel"--good news--is. Here our evangelism is often: "Do you know where you will be when you die?" That is not good news at all. --Burmese church leader*

then a series of tasks which arrive in the context of these two terms. The first word to be understood is, of course, "mission" itself. Often "mission" is used to describe the entire life and work of the church, that is "the mission of the church." Missiologists have criticized this use, referring to the oft-quoted dictum: "If everything is mission than nothing is mission." However, "mission" is probably the broadest of the terms to talk about the task of the church *in the world*. Mission has to do with sending and being sent. It can be said that mission is what God sends the church into the world to do. In making this statement it must be kept clearly in mind that the church is worldwide, and that God is everywhere. Thus sending in mission is a multi-directional process.

B. Service

The second word which must be understood is "service." It is of central importance to Christians that Jesus, who was sent by God into the world, was among humanity "as one who serves." The number and spread of references to servanthood in the Bible make it clear that this aspect of Christian life and witness must be taken very seriously. Some would say that service is a central facet of the church's mission in the world, as are evangelism and the witness for justice and peace. Others would say that service is half of a whole of which mission is the other half, or the flip side of the mission coin. However, to the writers it seems useful and biblical to think of service/servanthood--we will not enter here into the discussion over the respective meanings of these two terms--as a biblical call which is whole in its own right. This understanding implies that any aspect of mission--the "what?" or being sent-- is to be characterized by the spirit of service--the foundation of the "how?"

We have also recognized that the "service posture" is a way of life built deep into the fabric of many traditional cultures, and that often Christians in other parts of the world have grown up with cultural attitudes which value service more than do North American Christians.

Mission agencies in the west are separate from the church. So are service agencies. These dichotomies are incomprehensible to Middle Easterners, and heresy to Middle Eastern churches -- Middle Eastern church leader

The writers assume that the list of tasks found in the following points can all be understood from both the mission perspective--what Christians are sent to do--and the service perspective--the posture with which Christians take up their tasks.

C. Evangelism

Evangelism is an important and a complicated term in mission lexicon. It is sometimes used interchangeably with "evangelization"--but the latter term is usually used to define a certain style of evangelism. We define "evangelism" as proclamation about Jesus, his teachings and life, his death and resurrection, and as a call to the hearers to become followers of Jesus. The writers believe that evangelism is a central part of the mission of the body of Christ, but that it is only a part. In order for evangelism to make any sense, the persons involved must be able to invite those they meet into the church. It is a false concept of evangelism which only invites persons into an individual belief system. The church has to make sense both to those who are learning about Jesus and his followers for the first time, and to those who have heard about Jesus, observed his followers and decided in the past that they do not make sense.

The overwhelming sentiment of the informants to this project is that the work of evangelism is best done at a personal or small group level, by persons of the same or a neighboring culture to those to whom the message is being presented. The evidence the writers have is that this form of evangelism is really having the greatest impact. This understanding is often in conflict with much of the thinking of those who speak of world evangelization, whose perception is that any method that "works" is good, and that it is desirable to send people far away to very different environments in order to do the work of evangelism. The writers heard repeatedly that North American Mennonite agencies should devote their energy and resources for evangelism first of all to equip North Americans for evangelism in North America, and also to assist persons and churches in other parts of the world in equipping themselves for evangelism in their immediate or neighboring areas.

> *Too many churches boast about numbers at the expense of quality. Christians are too much in a hurry to evangelize the world that they don't lay a solid foundation and consequently too many people fail. --Zambian BIC Bible teacher*

Strategies and methods always reflect the culture in which they originated, including the values and presuppositions of that culture. We must be aware of this fact when strategies and methods are used cross-culturally and evaluate them in the light of several criteria: 1) Do they enhance respect for all people whatever their faith or ideology? 2) Do they build up the whole body of Christ rather than a particular group? 3) Do they contribute to the church's witness for justice, peace and the integrity of creation? 4) Do they avoid enticements which either seem to or actually do buy converts? The goal should always be to present the gospel as clearly and sensitively as possible so that the hearer can respond to that rather than to the values and standards of modern/western culture.

An important part of the modern call to evangelism comes from cosmopolitan, multi-cultural, modern, secular urban areas. The writers' experience is that there are connections and similarities between these centers wherever they are located throughout the world. Whether among drug addicts and prostitutes or university intellectuals, among wealthy industrialists or poor factory workers, these centers present the challenge of a post-Christian or post-religious world. North American Mennonites' experience in our own cities has been a difficult one. In order to consider carefully whether and where we are called to the task of evangelism in urban centers elsewhere around the world, we should begin conversations with those whose witness has stood the test of time. The writers were moved by many examples, including a coalition of evangelicals in inner city London linking house churches, a pastoral couple providing a home for addicts in Calcutta, and a church leader in

Nairobi who thinks of the new reality faced by the first generation of young Africans born in the city.

D. The church takes form

1. Church planting

Church planting has become the primary focus of many mission agencies throughout the world. This commitment takes seriously the need of individual believers to belong to a church community. It also emphasizes the centrality of the local congregation/fellowship as the basic building block of the broader church. However, the writers believe that as a task, church planting has been too simplistically and too singularly chosen as the focus for much North American mission activity. There are several problems with church planting as a focus as the writers observed it. First, church planting concentrates too narrowly on establishment of an immediate quantifiable structure, leaving to one side the matter of long-term nurture of the congregation, how new groups can provide the necessary support for the "marginal" people they almost inevitably attract early on, what kinds of witness beyond itself the congregation wishes to and should have, what the socio-economic and political realities are from which members come, with whom and how the congregation will belong. We also find the statement of "Biblical Values and Principles" outlined by International Urban Associates a powerful declaration of positive directions for urban witness, pulling together the many reflections we heard on the challenge of mission in the world's urban centers.

Second, church planting is almost always done according to western/northern models of congregational life and leadership. This leaves young congregations feeling lost and hopeless when western/northern personnel are withdrawn, and incapable of considering other models of congregational life. Mission agencies often support full-time western workers to plant the congregation, but expect the

> *Anglicans do not like church planting. We are the church in this place. Please come as part of the worldwide church in partnership with our church in the face of an enormous mission. --British leader in the Anglican church renewal movement*

group to carry on without subsidy when it becomes independent. In many cases the congregation cannot support their own full-time paid leaders. This experience detracts from the process of thinking about alternative models of congregational life, and tempts people to think that whatever they do to carry on their life together is inferior to what they were brought. The writers observed missionaries in Colombia wondering what would happen to their congregation when they left, and

12

talked with congregational leaders in Italy and Japan struggling after the departure of expatriate congregational leaders.

When the presence of expatriates leads to the formation of new congregations, questions of leadership and linkage must be addressed quickly. North Americans should not be alone in leadership in any such situations.

2. Nurture

Providing nurture for new believers in settings where the church is taking form is a difficult matter. Some churches, especially in the pentecostal-charismatic tradition, take the matter of nurture seriously and have laid out clear methods for providing it. It is the writers' observation that these structures often operate quite hierarchically. In other contexts, especially in places where Mennonite workers have been struggling to help a church take form, the issue of nurture is a critical one. When a congregation is small, and the core of "stable" members even smaller, it is difficult to find the stamina and wisdom to care for those with serious emotional, physical or family problems who are often attracted to such a new group. These realities seem especially pressing in urban settings.

Family life issues are particularly significant for new believers in many different settings. Often family members follow one another into a new

> *Many denominations have activities to bring people in, but not much to keep them. We need much love and the fruits of the Spirit to keep people. -- Venezuelan Mennonite woman*

congregation, bringing whatever family problems exist into the heart of the congregation. Marital and extra-marital relations and divorce are serious problems in churches almost everywhere. Polygamy continues to raise questions among African Christians. Psychological problems haunt many people in societies struggling with rapid and confusing change. Children who are rebellious, caught up in drug culture or new religious movements, or unemployed even if educated, cause their parents to carry heavy burdens.

The writers did not hear many recommendations on how to do better at offering nurture to young churches. Our observations were that it is very important for each small group to have a link to other groups in order to have a pool of pastoral resources to draw on. Advice from one urban church worker was that no church will stay alive without a committed core group of workers who are ready and able to carry such burdens. While rural issues for new churches may be quite different, it is quite likely that the need for a similar core community is equally strong. The writers believe that the matter of nurture in new congregations is one to which North American Mennonite agencies involved in their formation should give more study and attention.

3. Theological education/ leadership training

a. The need for leadership training. Training activities were perhaps the things the writers heard about and observed the most while visiting churches around the world (with development projects coming a close second). The greatest sense of

> In development work you say: "Don't give people fish, teach them to fish." It should be the same for mission work. Give people the Bible and the best education possible, and let them figure out what it means. --German-speaking Brazilian Mennonite

inadequacy and need were also expressed about theological and other training possibilities. National and local programs are being developed by denominations, interchurch groups and a host of independent agencies. Various training forms are in place--resident seminaries and Bible schools, extension seminary and Bible school training, theological education by extension for lay people, special seminars and short courses, small local group and individual study. Yet no one feels that enough is being done. The writers suggest that the haunting sense of not having enough trained leaders or opportunities for education/training is strongest where church people have thrown in their lot with the western/northern church, both its structures and its resources. We were struck with the story of the founder of an independent church in Benin, who gladly sent his church members to participate in the interchurch Bible training program, but who had before that developed his own internship system for training young leaders in preaching and Bible, with a strong sense that what he was doing was right, good and adequate. The writers believe that an increasing percentage of our personnel and financial resources should be given to the realm of developing various forms of leadership training and theological/biblical education, particularly to forms which build up initiatives which churches already have in place and feel ownership for. It is also essential to join Mennonite and interchurch groups in thinking about the various alternatives to meet the needs of their churches and people for this training.

b. Academic and practical training. In formal theological/biblical training programs, much more emphasis is needed on integrating practical concerns with academic concerns. This area is a topic of current discussion in North American as well as international institutions, and there are experimental models which could be studied by those who share the concern to offer better interdisciplinary study. Practical issues include experience in pastoring/leading a local congregation, youth activities, teaching, counseling, evangelism, being a body of believers in indifferent or hostile environments, choosing forms of witness, delegation of responsibility throughout the congregation, financial control and accountability, and methods of self support. Much more work is needed on models of local church leadership which assume whole or partial self-support. Because North Americans have almost entirely lost touch with this concept in the past generation, their role may be to unearth models being used elsewhere and to spread that information broadly among other churches.

c. **Other leadership needs.** In many places churches feel a serious lack of people in their midst with leadership skills other than those related directly to congregational leadership--administration, business management, legal training, health care and agriculture. Another leadership need in the church is translation. In Asia more people need to be equipped in English in order to facilitate conversation among themselves throughout the region. In Latin America there is more language unity, but in the church community there are indigenous people or those coming from English-speaking areas who do not speak Spanish or Portuguese. Throughout Africa there is great language diversity, but capacity in English, French and Portuguese should ease communication opportunities.

The writers believe that some North American financial resources should be available to provide training scholarships for people whose role in the local church is firmly established. Questions of where this takes place and what to do about the inevitably "brain-drain" loss of trained personnel must be asked, but should not rule out some form of cooperative effort at providing more training for church people around the world.

d. **Literature/audiovisual production and study centers.** Two specific needs call for greater involvement by North American Mennonite agencies. These needs are expressed by those involved in the tasks of evangelism, theological education and leadership training, the witness for justice and peace, and relief development. In a world of information explosion it is hard for North Americans to understand why the need for literature and audiovisual material on questions of the church and Christian faith, or for centers where people could gather to read and view such materials and discuss them with one another, is so critical. But the lack of such resources to Christians and persons exploring the Christian faith is severe in most other parts of the world. Churches need much more material produced in languages their people can use, whether books and pamphlets, cassette recordings or videos. In many places, especially in urban areas, students and young professionals are looking for places where they can study and talk and where materials are available to them. Visits to the American cultural center in any capital city offer one small sign of the demand for any such resources. The writers believe that North American Mennonite agencies should place a greater percentage of their resources, both financial and personnel, into literature and audiovisual production of materials particularly reflecting Mennonite understandings and perspectives, and into developing study centers.

E. Witness for justice, peace and the integrity of creation

It is the opinion of the writers that witness for justice, peace and the integrity of creation is a central part of the mission of the church in the world. There are clear calls from churches around the world for more, and more whole-hearted, North American participation in this form of Christian witness. There is critique of the tendency of North American agencies to compartmentalize this area of witness away from other parts of church life and work, or to see it as a witness for the specialized or the few. Christians in many parts of the world who do carry out such a witness feel lonely and lacking in support, and clearly call North Americans to stand alongside them. They place high value on "accompaniment" as a central mission task. Many Christians also point out that the whole mission in which North American Christians are involved is negatively affected by our reluctance or refusal to join in witness for justice, peace and the integrity of creation in North America itself. They further remind us of the devastating impact on North American mission and service efforts elsewhere of United States government foreign policy. We believe that the concept of "peace church evangelism" is particularly fruitful for North Americans to ponder further in light of international as well as domestic realities.

> We face failure, pressure, loneliness. To have God in our midst is very important. It seems to us very natural, very important, to have the struggle for justice and faith in Christ together. --Hong Kong Christian Industrial Committee worker

> Your mission is very important. There are no borders for Christians. You must say to those who think United States bombs and bullets are for a good cause that all such aid brings death. --El Salvadoran sister

F. Relief and development

North American Mennonites have given priority to meeting human need around the world. At present this takes the form of a highly visible separate North American agency (MCC) with responsibility for international relief and development tasks. Christian brothers and sisters in other parts of the world express both appreciation for the service of MCC workers and confusion about the North American need to separate out these tasks from other parts of the work of the church. Among ourselves, North American Mennonites have also experienced the tension which comes from placing different values on physical or material tasks and those considered to be spiritual tasks. Both North Americans and our partners in other places also agree that the structural separation of a service agency has at times allowed for creative responses by the churches to specific needs around the world.

Christians in many places recognize the painful reality of human need around them. Often they call North American Christians to join them in responding to that need. Sometimes the response takes the form of immediate physical input in times of crisis. At times the response takes the form of providing resources and technical advice to assist communities in increasing food production, health care, literacy, or housing.

In accordance with the New Testament record the writers believe that healing must be taken more seriously by western/northern Christians. Christians in Africa, Latin America and Asia all spoke to us about their understanding that Jesus heals in their settings today. Apart from institutional medical forms, healing is a gift that western/northern churches are minimally familiar with. The writers believe that we need to open ourselves to learn from other Christian traditions about the practice of the ministry of healing.

> *Mostly people are pulled into the church by the actions of Christians, because Christians have helped them. --Tanzanian pastor*

The results of North American relief and development efforts are usually judged as much by the servant stance of the workers involved as by the visible items which they leave behind. North American Christians must recognize that Christians in other places may respect and appreciate our presence in relief and development tasks but that they may also determine at times that the resources of their own communities alone come closer to meeting needs in the best way.

G. Within the broader Christian world

North American Mennonite mission and service workers need to take another look at the nature of their presence in settings where Roman Catholic, Orthodox or other than "evangelical" Protestant churches are important religious factors. The writers believe that the assumption of conflict between

> *I love the Mennonite brothers and sisters from North America, but I note that not all are willing to know the reality in which we live and work. Pastoral and missionary work has focused on proselytizing. The changes the Catholic Church is making should be carefully studied. We need to find out how we can extend our help to these changes. --Mexican Mennonite pastor*

Mennonite workers and other such Christians is inaccurate. We heard illustrations in Germany, Egypt, El Salvador and Botswana, to name a few places, of positive opportunities for witness when the Mennonite presence began from the perspective of respect for and desire for conversation with other Christians present in a given location. We believe that such models are the only acceptable ones for North American Mennonites, and that even when there are differences of perspective, we are not free to carry on our tasks of evangelism or forming new churches as if we were not in the presence of other followers of Christ.

H. Christian mission and other faiths

1. The importance of understanding and respect

There is a great deal of missiological discussion about whether and how Christians should witness among people of other faiths. Views range from the school of radical dialogue, seeking to move to a new spiritual reality which believers in different faiths can share together, to the school that develops aggressive methods to bring believers in other faiths to the point of conversion to Christianity and the visible forms of the church. To lay out a complete perspective on the Mennonite North American way of relating and witnessing to people of other faiths goes beyond the purview of this paper.

> In India it is not that people have not heard the gospel; they have, and have chosen not to believe. So the question is, "How does the church relate to these people and their religions?" People have chosen to remain in their traditional religions. --Sri Lankan pastor

However, the writers heard a great deal about the need for North American workers to have a good understanding of other faiths in settings where they serve, to respect the values of those faiths as well as the people who are committed to them, and to understand that mission tasks are understood differently by Christians whose next-door neighbors are believers in other faiths. The North American sense of call to any form of ministry or presence in places where other faiths are strong--especially where political-legal restrictions are added to social controls--needs to be tested through contact and conversation with local Christians. Our basic premise is that we respect legal and cultural restrictions and only choose to go around them after careful study, consultation and prayer. Christians/churches in nearby or similar settings should be included in this discussion, as should Mennonite or other sister western/northern agencies with interests in the area. Great care should be taken to assure that presence in such settings is undertaken clearly for the sake of the gospel and not for the thrill or fund-raising potential of such presence.

2. Looking for new mission/church models

North American mission and service personnel working in contexts where other faiths are active must begin:

a. to look more actively at alternative forms which allow people to be in a new community in a way which does not offend (or at least is more dialogical with) the traditional religio-cultural patterns.

> The language teacher in our high school is from a high-caste Hindu family. He believes in the Lord in his heart. But if he is baptized, his whole family will be destroyed. I used to think that such believers should come out openly, but now I accept them. We need to be more open to this way. --Indian Mennonite high school teacher

b. to seriously consider how the church can provide meaningful familial and cultural support systems to those who are forced out of their own families/cultures because of their decision to follow Christ.

c. to pay more attention to the ways in which people of all faiths share common values which call those overtaken by the modern lack of faith, or by new idolatries, to repentance and conversion.

3. Primal religions

Major world religions are not the only form of religious expression which are significant in our time. Primal religions, the belief systems of tribal/indigenous people, are widespread in many regions. There are many troubling links between conversion from "tribal" to "world" religion and the push or desire for modernization among people of traditional cultures. Christian missionaries and service workers need equal sensitivity and awareness in those

> Often tribal people do not see conflicts between Christian and tribal ways. Sometimes they adopt Christianity as a way into lowland culture. --Filipina church worker

environments as we do in settings where major religions are the most important factor.

4. Popular religions

Still another important modern religious reality is what is known as "folk" or "popular" religion. This is the particular blend of traditional beliefs and tenets of a "world" religion which often grows in a setting where people are in transition from traditional to modern society. Folk religion has been held in low esteem both by leaders of the majority religious system in place and outside missionaries. For example, there is widespread criticism of the spiritual value of fiesta processions of Central American Catholicism, or of the blend of sorcery and Koranic tradition in West African villages. However, the writers believe that folk religions provide strong indicators of the needs a people have at a particular time, and are not simply an inferior belief system. Mission and service workers in settings where folk religion is strong--whether in a Christian or in another religious stream--should begin by attempting to find what can be learned from people's practice of customs of folk religion.

IV. Personnel

A. Yes and No to North Americans

The primary motivation for the MISP was the Mennonite Church goal to double the number of North American Mennonite workers in international mission and service assignments. During interviews the writers listened carefully for the attitudes that Christians in other parts of the world have about whether and how North American workers should be present in those places. We heard both "yes" and "no" to the question about North American mission/service presence.

1. Yes, North American workers should come:
    a. if they are committed to Christ and to the building up of the church in every place.
    b. if they have demonstrated their capabilities at home in North America.
    c. as an expression of the universality of the body of Christ.
    d. if they can live sensitively and openly in the midst of other cultures and religions.

    People from outside can be living symbols of the worldwide church. This reality must be conditioned by the acceptance of outside Christians that the church is not only universal but local. -- Egyptian church leader

    e. to accompany us in the lonely struggle for justice.
    f. to provide technical expertise.
    g. to participate in various aspects of the work as outlined by the local/regional/national church.

2. No, North American workers should not come:
    a. when they are unwelcome or illegal in our political or religious milieu.

b.   because there are too many of them. We are being flooded with Americans.
c.   if they do not respect and work within our systems.
d.   if they have their plans and solutions already worked out.
e.   if they are agents of U.S. government policy.
f.   if they are culturally insensitive and arrogant.
g.   because they are too wealthy and need too much.

> American Christians' wealth and technology is daunting to Europeans, and overwhelming to others. --British woman church leader

It is clear that feelings are both strong and varied. Perhaps the most telling comments were those from people who explained all the reasons why North Americans were not welcome as mission and service workers, and then added: "But if they are like X, they should come," or, "But we are glad for Y. She does not seem like an American."

B. Sending Models

1. Exchange missioners

Organizations such as the World Council of Churches and the Council for World Mission have taken deliberate steps to move from a pattern of sending personnel from North to South to a model which "looks at

> We have a need for fellowship among the churches within Asia. We know more about the churches in North America than we do about those in Asia. --Indian technical school administrator

human resources from a worldwide perspective," according to one WCC staff person. In practical terms, this means organizing a structure which can send people from any part of the world to any other. A worker might be sent from the United Kingdom to an agricultural project in Zambia. A Japanese pastor might be sent to lead a congregation in Brazil. The intention is that decisions about the assignment of these workers are made by a group which represents all the participating churches as equal partners. Tasks range the spectrum of mission and service involvement.

2. Missionaries under the receiving church

Most western denominational mission agencies follow some variation of this model, and it is one part of the understanding which regulates the exchange process described above. The essential principle of this sending model is that workers who go out are requested, invited by, and under the direction of the church who receives them. Decisions about persons and tasks are usually made in consultation between the receiving church and representatives of the sending agency. This model is close to what most Mennonite mission agencies follow.

3. Internationalization

Internationalization takes at least three forms: a) an international agency or an agency with its original headquarters in one country sets up national boards to run its programs in countries or regions, and hires national or regional staff to carry out those programs (World Vision); b) an international agency begins with national offices in several countries and sends out staff from those countries to many other countries (Overseas Missionary Fellowship); c) an agency head-quartered in one country recruits people from other countries to assign in its programs. Work performed ranges the spectrum of mission and service tasks.

4. Increasing numbers

Mission agencies from North America and Europe, and from parts of Asia, Africa and Latin America as well, are working to increase the number of workers they send in cross-cultural mission (to another country or at least to a region where the people are of a different language and cultural origin from their own). These workers are usually responsible only or mainly to the sending structures, and their work tends to be defined as church planting or primary evangelism.

5. Short-term workers

Many different groups are arranging programs to send workers for short-term (3 weeks to one year) assignments in cross-cultural settings. Sending groups range from mission boards to individual congregations to agencies organized specifically for the purpose of short-term sending. Short-term workers can be involved in primary evangelism, in church-support areas such as literature distribution, or in community service such as work-camp projects.

6. Medium-term service secondment

While primarily used by secular and governmental agencies (such as International Voluntary Service or Danish Volunteers) this model is closest to MCC's working pattern. The agency sends/seconds workers to a variety of local organizations which request them to carry out programs of its own.

7. Nonresident workers

Under this model agencies of all kinds send persons to work for brief periods, especially into settings where it is not possible for them to work and reside on a long-term basis. A variety of patterns are included: open assignments, such as a teacher who spends a term in an institution, and covert assignments where workers go into a country with the pretense of business or tourism in order to carry out a task such as literature distribution or personal evangelism.

8. The writers understand from informants that there are drawbacks to all of these models. Exchange mission (model one), for example, can be cumbersome and deal only with internal, structural church needs. There are questions about how honest it is to say that western/northern missionaries are really *under* the receiving church. Western/northern agencies also sometimes chafe at the restrictions model two puts on their desire to build other local relationships or do things which the receiving church is uncomfortable about. Medium-term service secondment may seem to the host organizations or communities as lacking in structural accountability, and at times workers' terms are too short.

Nevertheless, the writers feel that existing North American agencies can profit by taking a new look at models one, two, five and six, and at ways in which positive aspects of these models can be incorporated into new patterns for personnel involvement. We also believe that North American agencies should begin to develop some nonresident worker assignments in conversation with church partners in places where other sending models are no longer acceptable.

C. Specific requests

Even though seeking specific assignment openings was not the purpose of the writers' travels, we heard a variety of specific ideas or unofficial requests for mission and service personnel from North America. In order to point out the spectrum of possibilities which could be explored, we list some of these requests below:

1. England: support staff (e.g. librarian) to Selly Oak Colleges
2. Netherlands: students for a year or two at the Mennonite seminary in Amsterdam
3. Spain: Bible teachers with the Filadelfia churches
4. France: Bible teachers/leadership partners among congregations of the French Mennonite Conference
5. Federal Republic of Germany: leadership partners for urban Mennonite congregations
6. Bahrain: medical staff for the American Mission Hospital
7. Thailand: translator for the Church of Christ in Thailand (CCT)
8. Indonesia: English-language assistant for the Indonesian Communion of Churches (DGI)
9. Hong Kong: long-term missionaries for people-oriented ministries
10. Korea: long-term workers willing to come and find their place
11. Jamaica: missionary to stand alongside the church

12. Burkina Faso: Bible teacher/church resource developer
13. Cote d'Ivoire: media (literature/radio) technician
14. Benin: agriculturalist
15. Nigeria: teachers, seminary teacher
16. Swaziland: Bible trainer
17. Zimbabwe: medical staff
18. Zambia: Bible teacher for independent churches
19. Zaire: administration and management trainer
20. Sudan: developer for university environmental science program

D. Characteristics of cross-cultural mission and service workers

1. Physical characteristics

a. Mission and service workers need to be in good physical health. This does not mean they must be in perfect health, or that they must never be ill. Nor does it mean that there is no place in cross-cultural work for anyone with physical disabilities.

b. Workers need to be able to deal both with illness which comes from a new environment and with different and at times apparently inadequate health care systems in the new setting. They need to be willing to be sick at times, especially while adjusting to a new climate and new "bugs."

> If God calls you to go to Peru, go and preach God's word, but do not criticize their culture. You must eat their food--and sleeping in their houses is the same thing. --Indigenous Argentine pastor

c. Workers need to be aware that it is possible to give great cultural offense by refusing to eat or drink certain things, or by behaving as if people from the host culture are unhealthy. It takes time to sort out ways to accept local hospitality without putting oneself at undue risk.

d. Workers need to develop skills in understanding their own bodies and providing home treatment for some illnesses about which they might quickly seek professional consultation if they were "at home." It is important for them to know when and where to go for medical help. Workers should be able to learn and profit from local health care practices and traditional wisdom.

e. North American workers also have to live with the reality that in some cases they are not able to accept health care options which local people have no choice but to accept. In planning for emergencies and long-term health care, workers must acknowledge that some of their needs are unjust. They must be honest in trying to draw a line on special treatment for themselves.

2. Educational characteristics

a. Mission and service workers need a skill, and in most cases it must be a practical skill. In order to satisfy immigration requirements in many countries they need to be equipped with at least a bachelors degree.

b. Workers also need to have the patience and willingness to do something different than what they feel skilled to do, or even to do nothing for a time, in order for the process of finding the local direction of their work to take place.

c. Workers need ability to use the tools of the social sciences-- anthropology, sociology, psychology. They should also be able to understand these tools as simply tools, and to avoid the temptation to rigidly quantify or pre-plan their work.

d. Workers need a good base in biblical studies and an understanding of Mennonite/Anabaptist history and distinctives.

e. Whatever their assignment, workers need to be prepared to take a role in the life and work of the church, to be able to share comfortably in preaching, teaching and praying.

f. Workers need to be capable of and willing to learn at least one other language. They need to understand that taking this task seriously and doing it well are primary indicators to others that they take a people and its culture seriously.

Mission candidates should know that, whatever they learned in seminary, they do not know enough. They should be willing to put their seminary knowledge aside to learn afresh from the country and people. --Tanzanian bishop

g. Workers need to be "trainable"--ready to recognize that they do not know everything necessary for the new environment and open to be taught by people locally. They need to be willing to submit skills and education acquired elsewhere to the retraining process of the local setting.

3. Psychological and emotional characteristics

a. Workers need to be reasonably comfortable with themselves.

b. Workers need to be flexible.

c. Workers need to be aware of their development into a bi-cultural personality, with the accompanying reality that they never again feel entirely at home anywhere.

d. Workers need to be willing to talk about their problems with local people they can trust.

e. Workers need to be patient with themselves and others.

f. Workers need to be willing to work in a team, whether with other expatriates, a mixed expatriate-local group, or a team entirely made up of local people.

4. Spiritual characteristics

a. Workers must believe in Jesus Christ and have a personal commitment to follow him.

b. They must be committed to the teachings of the Bible and willing to understand them in ways that go beyond the boundaries of the interpretations of their own culture.

c. Workers must be willing to take on the discipline of simplicity in life standards.

d. Workers need to have an attitude of repentance for personal failures in the mission context as well as on behalf of the history and experience of the people who came before them.

We need grassroots church planting, with a different theology: a base community approach that provides fellowship and a biblical critique of society. That is the strength of the Mennonites. -- Hong Kong church renewal leader

e. They must be willing to receive forgiveness from those in the new culture.

f. Workers should be committed to ministries of listening and hope.

g. They should actively seek for ways to be peacemakers, and to support however possible the struggle of local people who work for justice and peace.

h. Workers need to be open to a growing awareness of the work and presence of the Holy Spirit in and around them.

i. They must understand and relax in the truth that the work is God's, not theirs.

E. Training:
a proposal for short-term and longer-term mission workers

1. Growing up as world citizens

Many North American Mennonite mission and service workers point out that the first stirrings of interest in the world beyond their home and communities took place when they were young children. This interest was fanned by parents who opened homes to international guests, by family members who were sent out and returned from international assignments, and by churches which invited international guests and mission workers to speak.

Mennonite and interchurch agencies continually struggle to find good ways to inform churches in North America and encourage them to participate in mission around the world. Many creative mission and development education projects have been developed by the agencies in recent years. But often we do not feel very successful in efforts to inform people as broadly as possible, encourage better financial responses and call more of the right people into mission assignments.

North American Christians must recognize that mission education in North America--as well as mission practice in other parts of the world-- will often conflict with the understandings and behaviors of our own society and culture. But adults who model alternatives joyfully and children who have a chance to learn-by-doing while minds are still open are important resources who continue to be present in our congregations. The writers believe that it can be an exciting challenge for North American Christians to hear new calls to incarnational witness. We can be enthusiastic about making visible links between the North American mission task and the task in other parts of the world, about supporting efforts that we share with others rather than control alone, and about sending people to learn from the faith of others as well as to share their own.

2. Short-term cross-cultural learning-exchange opportunities

In almost all settings the writers heard the desire for more opportunity to exchange ideas about mission, church life, and how faith affects culture, between Christians from the west/north and Christians from the east/south. In their comments on North American Mennonite youth programs, informants offered positive evaluations when such programs were viewed as opportunities for North American young people to learn or for mutual encouragement in the church. Evaluations were negative in cases where the programs were seen as mission/service from North America. We believe that all of the short-term mission and service programs now organized by North American Mennonite agencies should be restructured to include exchange dimensions. All of the models listed below should also be seen as potential opportunities for training/internship for those who might become involved in longer-term assignments. The training components noted are mainly with North American participants in view.

> We do not have a Goshen College where North American Mennonites can send their children to study, but we would be honored to see their children study in our universities, founded and recognized well ahead of Harvard. --French Mennonite leader

a. Youth Programs: mission internships, IVEP, Inter-Menno, SALT, YES (six months to one year). Training would include background reading, orientation, in-country orientation through local sponsors, post-term debriefing.

b. Study abroad: Brethren Colleges Abroad, SST, specialized opportunities such as Yonsei University in Korea or Daystar University College in Kenya (three months to one year). Training would include background reading, the study opportunities on location, language learning and post-term debriefing.

   c. **Learning tours:** (three to five weeks). Training would include background reading, brief orientation, on-location contacts and discussion and debriefing.

   d. **Cross-cultural voluntary service opportunities:** for example, first-term MCC (two to three years). Training would include an undergraduate degree, specialized short-term training (Washington seminar, rural farm exposure), orientation, in-country orientation in care of the local church or other group (including "live-in" and language learning), on-the-job learning and debriefing.

3. Moving into longer-term commitment

The writers believe that a long-term international mission or service placement should rarely be made before the worker has experienced at least one of the above-listed short-term internship possibilities, or a related experience in North America. We believe that those with such experience should be considered the first priority pool from which long-term workers are drawn. The individuals themselves, their home churches, local churches where they lived and worked, and mission or service agencies should discuss persons' interest and aptitude together. Home church, local or national church, or agency mentors should take a much stronger role in "shoulder tapping" persons whose internship experience has made gifts in cross-cultural ministry clear. All should be encouraged to understand this process as one which calls for more than individual decision-making.

4. Inter-term training

Those who have completed the exchange/internship experience and for whom there is mutual agreement about continuing in international mission and service will at some point need additional training and in-service enrichment.

   a. Some of this training will come from ongoing orientation and seminars/refreshers by the sponsoring agency. An important area which needs greater attention in this training context is the fact that many long-term workers have the formal or informal role as liaison with local or national churches. Workers need help in determining appropriate ways to live out the liaison role.

   b. Seminary training: Only in exceptional cases should persons complete more than one term without spending a period of study in a Mennonite seminary or college. The various mission training center systems attached to these institutions should be beefed up in order to provide clear and individualized attention to planning programs for study and reflection for workers between terms. Some workers will feel strong urges to study in well-known missiological centers. Workers should be encouraged, even pushed, to enter missiological programs which reflect different Christian perspectives from the ones with which they are most familiar. (For example, Fuller people might spend time at Bossey or Maryknoll; Harvard people might spend time at Asbury.) Careful attention should be given to sending workers for periods of additional training in international seminary settings--San Jose, Pune, Bangui, Selly Oak, East Berlin, and so forth.

c. Where an assignment calls for additional technical training, efforts should be made to find institutions which offer good opportunities for integrated discipline study and further church relationship and participation.

d. Since competence in language is one of the most highly valued characteristics of mission and service workers, agencies should assure that opportunities for further language/linguistics training are provided for all workers. Differing gifts in this area must be acknowledged, but all persons who are called to long-term mission and service work need to accept the discipline of continuing language learning.

5. Length of assignment

Decisions about when and how long-term assignments of North Americans are completed should be made through a process of periodic consultation between the workers, the local or regional receiving church and the North American agency.

V. Money and structure

A. Mission and economic power

The mission and service agency structures through which North Americans work have grown out of models which emerged during the nineteenth century in Europe and United States, for mission agencies, and after the first world war, for service agencies. These models assume a western/northern base and decision-making group, resources coming from the expanding economic power of the societies and churches in which they spring, and a major involvement in tasks far away from the sources of money and people. Churches in other parts of the world are now developing mission structures based on similar models. It is the observation of the writers that western-based models assume a high degree of economic power, or at least more wealth and power among the senders than among those to whom they are sent. Such assumptions hold both internally for the church/agency and externally for the country or region where the church/agency is located.

Unfortunately the evangelical international enterprise is still subject to the spirit of colonialism. --Yugoslav Pentecostal professor

You put me in an impossible position when you ask for my vision--and you are the ones who have the money. The one who pays the piper calls the tune. -- Argentine Mennonite pastor

There are other models of mission and service, both historical and modern. However, these models have seldom been taken seriously by the church at large; they are not based on a need for promotion; in fact they would not be thought of by those involved as "models," but rather as a more natural way of expressing faith in life. We learned, for example, of congregations in the United Evangelical Church (indigenous Argentines) who have three pastors, so that the local work can always carry on when one or two of the pastors are moved by the Holy Spirit to travel away and evangelize.

Some of our young people dedicated themselves to go with only a few belongings to China to witness. They thought they would be killed, but God blessed them. -- Burmese pastor

The writers do not deny that God has been able to work, and that the church has been built through mission and service efforts which grew out of economically powerful churches and societies. But we suggest that the relational and task-oriented dilemmas which plague North American agencies today--in this we belong to a much larger church reality--come in large part because of the power/resource base from which we have worked and continue to work. North Americans are beginning to understand that the church is growing quickly in other parts of the world, and that the balance of Christian presence is shifting from North to South. There are many factors which cause this growth. In certain places and cases church leaders worry that growth is motivated by the perception that becoming a Christian makes it possible for a person to tap into the church's or some missionaries' apparent economic power. In other cases growth occurs because the church's message speaks to the realities of the lives of poor people.

Whatever the case, it is exceedingly uncomfortable to recognize that the church is growing elsewhere, but the economic resources are still mostly in western/northern hands. Some churches have tried to deal with this discomfort by choosing "the preferential option for the poor." Yet in several meetings where the writers heard this idea discussed, Christians admitted that we are still thinking we-they (church rich--other poor). Is it possible for a financially rich church to really give up some of its riches for the unfettered use of a financially poor church? What can rich and poor churches together do about the fact that, while a shift of economic balance in the world church is called for, the presence of financial resources can easily become a corrupting and negating influence rather than one which enhances the financially poor church's call to mission? To the writers, these are the most painful and least answerable questions which arise out of this study project. In the rest of section V below, the writers point out several areas which must be worked on in order to begin finding answers to money and structure questions.

B. Money or people

Western/northern mission and service agency patterns in modern times have been personnel intensive. Agencies exist to send out people who will do the work of evangelism, help a church take form, and provide the helping ministries which each situation calls for. It is true that large amounts of financial resources have often followed these people around the world. It is only necessary to visit the historic Mennonite mission stations--not to mention an inter-church theological institution here or there--to see how much money has been put into building up the infrastructure. However, the writers maintain that people have been at the heart of

> *It is easier for Western mission boards to second a person than to provide the funding. We are not minimizing the importance of partnership or personnel, but we are longing for the day when the majority of our full-time staff are national. --Egyptian seminary president*

the western/northern vision for mission. When the writers posed to two of the agencies supporting this project the question of how much of the international mission/service budget was spent for the support and maintenance of personnel, we were told that the answer was very hard to determine. One person said: "I have never been asked that question before." However, in both cases the consensus was that personnel support takes up a greater percentage of the international budget than any other single item.

Almost all Christians in other parts of the world find it very disturbing that western/northern mission/service agencies are apparently much more willing to put their money into our own personnel than anything else. In the Mennonite experience, questions about this are tied to the fact that the church has seen its options diminish as "independence" has come and western/northern personnel have been withdrawn. The writers believe that despite painful past experience, North American Mennonite agencies must take another look at the matter of providing funds to directly support church workers in other countries.

> *The work that missionaries did depended on their means. Now we do not have those means. Evangelism used to be done by car and now it is done by bicycle. --Zairean Mennonite pastor*

C. Decentralizing monetary structures

Western/northern financial managers want to enhance control and avoid chaos, and those working in mission and service agencies are no exception. The sense of responsibility for good stewardship and adequate reporting on use of contributions is a heavy one. While there are certainly other reasons why Mennonite agencies set up budget and fiscal policies as we do, these are central when we begin to talk about trying to find ways to release more financial resources to the control and use of churches elsewhere.

In addition, as noted above, North American Mennonite agencies all operate on the assumption that we are not financial donors. Yet all do provide funding for a variety of projects, usually discussed on a case-by-case basis with a specific partner. Church partners in other parts of the world find the process of discussing funding needs with North American agencies very complicated and difficult. In addition, partner churches would welcome North American participation in studying the realm of international interchurch project funding to understand how it works, what the advantages and disadvantages of participating in it are, and whether and when North American agencies can serve as a channel or a support to partner churches who wish to carry out a particular project with such funding.

There are several models North American Mennonite agencies use for transferring financial resources from North America to partner groups in other parts of the world. Currently we operate for the most part as individual agencies which make financial decisions related to tasks we are carrying out with one partner or a group of partners elsewhere. There also times when we opt for other more cooperative models. These models are described briefly below:

1. A North American agency provides funds for personnel and a variety of tasks taken on in discussion with one partner church or group.

2. A North American agency provides funds for personnel and a variety of tasks taken on in discussion with several churches or some other national or regional cooperative group.

3. Two or more North American agencies cooperate in funding a special project in discussion with a group of churches or other partners.

The writers suggest that all of the above models may be appropriate, but only or almost always for personnel and carrying out specific tasks which are seen as the core of one agency's call. We suggest that, among the variety of mission tasks, some be taken out of a direct bilateral decision-making relationship in order to be discussed and decided on in a non-North American forum. This process might be modeled in the following ways:

4. North American Mennonite Church agencies release money for a selected area of work to a fund whose use would be determined by representatives of a national or regional interchurch group in another part of the world together with designated North American representatives.

5. All North American Mennonite agencies with relationships in a given country or region (with an invitation to interested European Mennonite agencies) release money for a selected area of work to a fund whose use would be determined by a group including representa-

tives of all Mennonite groups in that country or region and representatives designated by the North American agencies.

6. All North American Mennonite agencies with relationships in a given region or continent release money to a fund to support exchange of church personnel within that region or continent, with decisions about use of the fund to be made by a regional or continental interchurch group.

All of the proposals in the second cluster assume relationships primarily between Mennonite churches. In situations where North American Mennonite agencies have relationships with other non-Mennonite churches, those relationships are probably best continued under model three of the first cluster, with care taken to assure increasing levels of accountability and information sharing.

The writers also assume that bilateral relationships between one North American agency and one international church partner may continue, but that that relationship should focus on a smaller and more specific set of tasks and personnel needs. It should also be a relationship which always encouraged interchurch cooperation at the local level.

Many North American mission workers, apart from those in short-term exchanges, may continue to be assigned through bilateral agency-to-church systems (as in financial models in the first cluster). The writers believe, however, that the decision-making structures of models four and five in the second cluster can become the predominant structures for assignment of some long-term North American personnel as well.

In all monetary relationships, the writers urge an increasing degree of openness by North Americans about what resources we have available, how we are willing to use them, and what decision-making processes we use. We also urge that as multilateral relationships develop, the question of monetary participation in specific projects by all members of the partnership be encouraged.

It is the writers' understanding that North American agencies will continue to be North American agencies rather than trying to internationalize *our* structures. The vision of the writers is to find ways to relax northern/western control over our resources as a means of entering into more fruitful and mutual partnership with churches and interchurch groups in other places.

D. Self-support

Most of the churches North American agencies relate to struggle to be self-supporting. The brave goals that the mature church should be self-governing, self-propagating and self-supporting have most frequently come to grief on the last point. Many Mennonite churches are very small (number of members). Many are living in settings where the overall economic situation is deteriorating. Many are experiencing problems because some members lack confidence in the leaders and hence do not contribute to support church structures. Many are burdened by responsibilities which were taken on during the time of western/northern mission control--for example, administration of hospitals and schools--which sap their energy for other church-related tasks. In some cases these same churches are facing renewed pressure from governments to continue or reassume such responsibilities because the governments themselves lack the resources to do so. Many have experienced the failure of self-support schemes such as farms and certain service institutions. Many are frustrated by the western/northern agency approach which views subsidies as undesirable and seeks to reduce them to zero in order to assure the "independence" of the partner church.

The writers believe, as noted above, that North American agencies should be prepared to provide some continuing subsidies to partner churches especially for areas that relate to the church's task of outreach or for cooperative interchurch projects. In addition, North American agencies must begin together with church partners and other local experts to study potential methods for increasing the ability of churches to support themselves. This study would include considering whether and when *projects* can be means of self-support and when other kinds of long-term, income-generating investments are more appropriate. North American agencies must provide more opportunities for management training and interchurch discussion about management and financial ethics in the church. We must further give more attention to helping congregations to develop their own bases of support, and to promoting greater south-south and regional discussion on models of self-supporting church leadership.

> *I do not agree with the mission boards' policy of reducing subsidies to zero. If the boards cut out all our support, I cannot imagine what will happen. There should be terms of agreement for a continuing contribution of a certain percentage--how much is not important--as a sign of mutual support in the church. -- Indonesian Mennonite mission administrator*

E. North American agencies and the church

One of the central incongruities of North American mission and service efforts is that the task is carried out by specialized agencies. While mission agencies for us are clearly denominationally/conference-tied, quite often they came into being through the pressure of church members who saw the need rather than by a decision of conference structures themselves. Now that there are churches in other parts of the world which have grown up through the efforts of Mennonite mission agencies, they are faced with the strange situation of continuing to relate, not to a church in North America, but to a church agency. The writers believe that it is important to find ways to increase the level of church-to-church discussion and planning together. This should not detract from the mission agency's ongoing commitment to a core task which the church has given to it. We believe that the pattern of Eastern Mennonite Board and Virginia Mennonite Board to name a church leader to develop an ongoing relationship with the church in each region or country where the board works is one model worthy of further consideration.

All of the North American agencies work to enhance congregational understanding of and support for the mission and service tasks they are carrying out. At times the agencies, and the denominational structures themselves, may forget that the congregations are the basic unit of the church for carrying out all its tasks--evangelism, witness for peace, and so on. Often agency structures find themselves attempting to stave off the efforts of North American congregations to get more directly involved in the mission and service work of the church in other parts of the world. The writers believe that North American Mennonite agencies should direct their attention to increasing opportunities for congregation-to-congregation contact, exchange, and international resource support between churches in North America and those in other parts of the world. Those responsible for such exchange would be responsible for:

1. assistance in finding a congregation or a cluster of congregations from another part of the world for a North American congregation or cluster of congregations to relate to; assistance in setting up channels of communication between the two;

2. information regarding what agencies are already doing together with the churches to which partner congregations belong;

If individual friends want to send us a gift, why do they have to go through the mission board office? Is the board taking out a percentage for their own costs? Such questions hang over our heads. -- Tanzanian Mennonite elder

3. assistance in planning mutual visiting;

4. trouble-shooting and providing advice when misunderstandings erupt;

5. encouragement to congregations to maintain giving to the agencies they support and to see direct congregation-to-congregation involvement as an additional opportunity to share.

F. North American inter-agency relationship

At a 1987 Consultation on Ministry in Global Perspective convened by the Council of International Ministries, the findings committee called for the establishment of "a task force to develop a proposal for increased cooperative overseas mission/service programs. This task force is expected to consult with non-North American churches in both the design and implementation of the regional/global mission task." To the writers' knowledge no steps have been taken in this direction. We underline that many of the ideas contained in this report can only move ahead if there is serious commitment to inter-Mennonite agency cooperation beyond that which now occurs in North America. Further, this report's recommendations are based on the hope that regional inter-Mennonite cooperation in other parts of the world can be strengthened.

The writers believe that Mennonite Church agencies should strongly urge CIM to take steps to bring such a task force into being, and be the first to offer wholehearted cooperation with it.

We further believe that the process begun through this two-year project--the process of non-administrative listening to Christians in various parts of the world--should be an ongoing one, involving people from other parts of the world in the listening and recording process. We believe that such a process can help to determine the shape inter-Mennonite cooperation in many places should take. We urge this task force to ask Mennonite World Conference to cooperate with it in bringing such a process into being.

VI. On Mennonite identity and mission

A. Current situation of the church in the world

Christian researchers are trying to define the current situation of the church in the world as well as the trends that are carrying the church into the future. Many of our informants also described the situation of the church in their environments, giving the writers a series of impressions about the shape of the global church realities at the beginning of the 1990s. Following is a list of these impressions:

1. Historic Protestant denominations in most places are struggling with declining membership and the internal and external critique of lifelessness. In some parts of the world this decline at an institutional level is counteracted by a host of small renewal groups who seek to bring together denominational identity with openness to new forms and theological understandings.

2. Christian people in general are coming together in new ways, relaxing ties of loyalty to historic churches and meeting around common practices and beliefs, such as charismatic-pentecostal worship or methods of evangelism, or around common issues such as the drug problem or anti-nuclear protest.

3. New non-denominational churches are forming everywhere from Lancaster County, Pennsylvania, to Bangalore, India, with picturesque names such as Catholic Good News Organization, Jesus Saves Gospel Temple, Missionary Bible Church, Holy Ghost Revelation Evangelical Fellowship Church, The Arm of the Lord Mission, and so forth. At times these churches are the result of a particular split from a previously existing church group, and at other times they grow more gradually through people following a charismatic leader.

4. In many areas Christians have the feeling that their communities are flooded with missionaries who have links neither to any group locally nor to any church body beyond a congregation in their sending

country. The majority of these missionaries are westerners/northerners, but more of them are now coming from other parts of the world.

5.   Many parachurch agencies are springing up, with funding from western/northern Christian groups outside historical church structures. These agencies draw talented leaders away from local churches and offer training programs that are better resourced than those that local or national churches can offer.

6.   In many settings it is easy to gather a crowd for a rally, a concert or another special Christian event, but it is extremely difficult to get those who attend to connect that event with a long-term commitment to a local church.

7.   International interchurch or inter-Christian structures of various theological stances maintain high-profile bureaucracies and hold visible gatherings. Those who are active in these structures represent a cosmopolitan elite who may have more in common with each other than with the national or local churches from which they come.

8.   Religio-political fundamentalism has had an impact on churches in many places, leading Christians to tie personal beliefs to commitment to political systems, especially those that are avowedly militaristic and anti-communist.

9.   Churches everywhere are reported to be growing. It is not clear how much of that growth is movement from church to church, and how the trend in Christian churches compares to apparent growth trends in other major world religions and new religious movements.

B. How we see ourselves and how others see us

Mennonites in North America in the 1990s are a very diverse group of people. We have among us those who are struggling over the matter of identity, and what the common themes are that we all respond to. The matter of identity is a critical one for the definition of our mission and service tasks. In general we believe that we are not part of the ecumenical movement--yet some of our most fruitful mission efforts and some of our most profound mission learnings have come in settings where we have been open to and participants in interchurch work. Most of us believe we are evangelicals; we have accepted this label without defining it too clearly but know it has something to do with holding to the uniqueness of Jesus Christ and taking the Bible absolutely seriously. Some of us speak of the third way and use the label Anabaptist but are not sure how the sixteenth century expression of faith affects the people we have become 400 years later. We struggle with the tensions arising because our missionary movement was born and grew almost entirely before we had rediscovered the Anabaptist vision.

Among church partners in other parts of the world, there is both frustration and admiration about things Mennonite. In many cases, the churches which grew up around Mennonite mission efforts see us as wealthy northerners who continue to hold the strings, either controlling their use of our resources or choosing unilaterally to withdraw those resources. They also feel buffeted about by changes in our mission policy and practice which they do not understand. Some Mennonite churches in Africa and Asia wonder why the Mennonite/Anabaptist identity is important when it was not mentioned by the early missionaries. In Central America some Mennonites have adopted the Mennonite/Anabaptist heritage because its biblical perspectives speak directly to their own historical-political context. They wonder why North American workers are so tentative in their own commitment to such biblical understandings.

> *It is by chance that we are Mennonites. We cannot refuse to accept that history now, but we shouldn't try to be identical to Mennonites in the west. We have our culture. We must be Zairean Mennonites. --Zairean Mennonite pastor*

Other churches who have worked with North American Mennonites or heard about our mission and service work have a happier perspective of our identity. Through the books written by Mennonite authors (*More With Less Cookbook, The Politics of Jesus, Christ and Violence, Christian Mission and Social Justice*) or through Mennonite workers who have lived in their midst, they believe that Mennonites have something to share with the broader church as it seeks to live and witness in the world.

> *No Mennonite missionary who has been to our country came as a committed Anabaptist. They learned those ways of living here. We are at a point where we must be Mennonites or we will be nothing. --Guatemalan Mennonite pastor*

C. The whole of mission and our particular gifts

In seeking tasks for North American Mennonites for the next decade, the writers have been reminded, we need to look first of all to the Bible and to the leading of the Holy Spirit through prayer. The writers believe that often the voices of Christians and other friends around the world can in fact be the moving of the Holy Spirit, and can help us to a new understanding of what the Bible says. We have clearly heard many Christians saying that North American Mennonites have something to offer the church at large. Our gifts have been named: commitment to simplicity, commitment to the Bible, readiness to follow Christ in life, a history of suffering, commitment to the witness for justice and peace, willingness to be servants, and commitment to whatever expression of the local church we find where we are sent. We believe the work of evangelism can be carried out in the context of exercising such gifts. We also understand that such gifts will be used by other Christians if Mennonites are no longer able and willing to do so.

The question can be raised about whether these gifts have any place in our relationships with sister churches which grew up around our mission efforts. The writers believe they do, beginning first of all with acts of repentance for failing so often to live out our gifts among these

There is beauty, freedom and flexibility in your smallness. You Mennonites can go where angels fear to tread. The question of peace and witnessing to the power of the cross are absolutely crucial in Thailand today. --Thai Christian social activist

sister churches and in our own environment. We believe that North American Mennonites must demonstrate these gifts in North America first of all. If we are willing to take the consequences at home for the witness of exercising such gifts, discussion with sister churches about how our understandings of the Bible and teachings of Jesus have changed will be more convincing.

D. A new challenge for Mennonites

In light of the insights and questions raised in sections A through C above, the writers do not believe that in the next decades the primary North American effort in other parts of the world should be to build more Mennonite churches. There will continue to be places where groups will grow up around mission and service efforts in which we participate, especially together with Mennonite churches from other parts of the world, and these groups will choose Mennonite identity. But in most cases North Americans should put our energy into supporting inter-church efforts to bring new churches into being. The efforts which we believe have greatest credibility for the overall Christian witness are those whose presence is clearly rooted locally but with an understanding of connections to the church around the world. They should be more defined by the need to meet the world of unfaith in

Our dream of urban work would not be denominational. It would be different Christians working together. --French Mennonite pastor

What is the reason to hold on to Mennonite identity? Does it mean something for our time? In a small world, which banner do we raise, Mennonitism or Christ? -- Indonesian Mennonite seminary teacher

positive confrontation and less defined by historical theological rigidities. They should be respectful of the richness of denominational pasts

42

and ever ready to draw on the strengths of those traditions, but willing to allow the new church to take shape in its own way and to shape those traditions to the realities of its own context.

In practical terms, the writers believe that North American Mennonites are called to and have the gifts for supporting church renewal movements in many places, and for working together with other local and outside denominations to build churches in the challenging parts of the world where they are needed. The exciting opportunities for North American Mennonite presence in other parts of the world will be both tied to the past and to the visible church, and to new forms and witnesses breaking out beyond the known.

> *We need people like the Mennonites here who try to help Christians regardless of their label. They ask: "Is this something which would strengthen the body of Christ in this town or region?"*
> *--Yugoslav Christian student worker*

E. The role of the international confessional body

It is not within the assignment of the MISP to comment on the international confessional body for Mennonites, the Mennonite World Conference. However, because of the nature of many of our conversations and the suggestions and ideas which have grown from them, the writers have found ourselves continually reflecting on the meaning of the MWC. The following ideas are offered not as critiques or program recommendations, but as an opportunity for further discussion about how the international Mennonite family participates together in mission. MWC has performed a number of very important roles. It has helped western/northern Mennonites to physically understand that the church is worldwide. MWC had made it possible for small and struggling churches around the world to realize that they belong to something bigger than themselves. It has promoted significant discussion on mutuality in mission and the nature of the peace witness. It has provided a forum for provocative Mennonites to throw out ideas which challenge and beckon the church at large. It has planted the seed of regional Mennonite cooperation for church life and growth.

MWC has also created problems for Mennonite churches worldwide. It has helped create an elite group of leaders who know one another and are comfortable functioning at an international level, while providing few handles on how to connect that international circle to church realities at the local level. Its most visible form of expression has been the every-six-years conference, an event accessible only to a few beyond wealthy North American and European participants. It has encouraged fledgling churches to take on the Mennonite identity for statistical and meeting purposes, when the motivation for such identification is not yet clear enough.

The writers believe that MWC has an important ongoing contribution to make to positive growth of the church and healthy understanding of the Mennonite identity. We believe that a much greater percentage of MWC energy and resource should go into developing the regional inter-Mennonite groupings. Such regional groups--Asia Mennonite Conference, for example--provide an important place to work out how to achieve the goals of the churches in mission. These groups provide a place for discussion of gospel and culture in a context where there is greater similarity of cultural issues than in an international body. They encourage a balance between an emphasis on Mennonite Christian identity and more awareness of regional similarities in culture, history and religious heritage. They provide a way for churches, some of which are very small, to gain enough power to function more equally as partners with western/northern mission agencies and churches. They provide a structural framework possibility for making changes in the flow of personnel and monetary resources, and for redefining who controls decision-making about such resources. They make participation in the confessional group less of a "plum" and more of a means to work on issues which truly affect the churches on a regular basis.

In some regions it may be most useful for an entire region to develop one structure. In others, for example in Latin America, smaller clusters of churches might best be able to work together (for example, Central America, the Caribbean, the Andean region and the Southern Cone). At a regional level Mennonite churches could be encouraged to think of what they have to offer to, and how they can participate with, the broader church in their region.

MWC's own serious difficulty with funding cannot be taken lightly. How is MWC to be able to facilitate such development? The writers believe that it is almost always--if not always--better to work cooperatively at all the tasks of mission. Thus we urge the North American agencies and churches, as well as churches in other parts of the world, to give higher priority to their contributions to MWC than to developing more advanced bilateral relationships between a North American body and one church in another place. For example, we would choose to place resources in an Africa Inter-Mennonite and Brethren in Christ Fellowship discussion about what kind of witness they might have in Southern

We need more communication within Latin America as Mennonites. We need to talk about the situations we find ourselves in today. We are like an island, isolated from other sisters and brothers. --Colombian Mennonite pastor

Africa before a conversation between Eastern Mennonite Board and the Tanzania Mennonite Church about sending workers to Mozambique. While the latter might be more concrete and immediate, we believe that the process of African Christians discerning the call together would lead to forms of mission which truly reflect the mutual nature of the church and allow many gifts within the body to be used.

VII. Other issues

There are a host of other issues which could be discussed in the context of a project such as this. Here the writers note a few which have especially impressed us and seemed to call for attention that could not be given elsewhere in the text of this report.

A. Indigenous peoples

There are an estimated 200 million indigenous peoples throughout the world, or approximately four percent of the global population. While there is no universally accepted definition for indigenous people, in general they are:

1. Descendants of original inhabitants of land colonized by foreign invaders.

2. People who consider themselves distinct people with their own ancestral territories, social values, and cultural traditions.

3. People whose existence as a distinct group is threatened.

Indigenous people are struggling for survival in North America, Latin America, Asia and Oceania. In Africa certain aspects of the majority cultures bear characteristics of indigenous peoples, as well as particular groups such as nomadic pastoralists, pygmies, and the Southern African San which are threatened.

Christian churches and missions have intersected with indigenous peoples in different ways. In the Americas, Christian missions on the whole were part of the brutal colonization which decimated indigenous populations. Indigenous peoples who became part of the church have appeared to others as deprived of culture and survival skills and forced into dependency on the charity of outsiders. In parts of Asia, on the other hand, Christianity has been accepted much more broadly by indigenous people than by the mainstream cultures. Hence the church, which is composed of a tiny minority of Asia's people, is also often a church composed of tiny minorities.

At present there are also different Christian responses to indigenous peoples. In some settings there are calls for renewed efforts to evangelize and plant churches in the midst of these groups still considered "unreached peoples." In other settings there is active church participation in the struggle for indigenous rights and even repudiation of evangelism efforts among such peoples. These responses make questions about Mennonite involvement among indigenous peoples particularly sensitive and urgent.

Mennonites have had experiences among indigenous peoples in Canada, United States, Central and South America, India, southern and eastern Africa. In several settings there are now indigenous churches which participate as members in Mennonite World Conference. These experiences have often been painful and at times positive. The writers believe that these experiences should be looked at and the wisdom of Mennonites and friends who have been involved should be tapped. Learning from such experiences should be brought together in such a way that they

> *Our message to you is that we are continuing in the way we learned about Jesus--that God loves both the Mennonites and us, and that we are all equal. --Paraguayan Lengua (indigenous) church leader*

can have an impact both on ongoing mission/services presence among indigenous peoples and on any other discussion Mennonite mission and service agencies might have about involvement with any "unreached peoples."

B. Women

Despite the writers' good intentions, we found it difficult in many places to have interviews with women. At times women were not present in meetings. At times they were present in the background, busy with the arrangements for hosting us--cooking, serving food or preparing beds. At other times, they were included in interview sessions, but men answered questions for them even when the questions were directed to the women. Occasionally when we met with women alone we were hindered by their shyness or our lack of ability in their languages. Yet many of the women we talked to spoke clearly, with wisdom and refreshing perspectives.

In every place, we heard that women are the heart of the church at the congregational level. They are the people who attend worship services regularly and bring children to church. Women do most of the work of primary evangelism with their neighbors. In African settings we also heard of women going in groups to visit and witness in areas farther away from their villages. Women function practically as deacons, arranging for material assistance and moral support for Christians and other neighbors going through times of crisis. Often women contribute a large percentage of the congregation's budget.

In some places women have their own organizations within the overall church structure. Only in rare cases do they take leadership roles in the church as a whole. There are at least two reasons for this. One is the fact that most church people are closed to the involvement of women in such roles. The other is that the demands on women to provide for the needs of their families are so great that they have no extra time for formal church work.

> *The pastor asked me: "Mama, why do we have women's groups?" I said, "We have women's groups to build up the church. Could you as a pastor deal with all those problems alone?" --Zairean Mennonite woman*

The writers believe that all North Americans involved in mission and service internationally must be aware of the significance of women's roles in the churches we relate to, and begin by publicly acknowledging these roles and expressing gratitude for them. Agencies should give high priority to making resources available to women, including finding income-earning possibilities, offering literacy training and assuring that there are good materials to read, working with women to develop programs of family life education in the realization that it is very often in family issues that the conflict of faith and culture come most strongly, and arranging possibilities for exchange. North Americans should also assist in pushing gently on church systems everywhere to include women at various levels of church work, and should do everything possible in our own lives and work to model positive, respectful and holistic involvement of women.

C. Youth

An African friend pointed out after reading through all four of the writers' continental reports that we had said very little either about young people *in* the church or about the need to invite young people to faith and the church. We realized in searching back through interview records how seldom we had talked to young people, and concluded that his observation was accurate.

We did hear Christians talking about young people, particularly their concern about unemployment and lack of educational opportunities. In other cases people spoke of pressure

> *Young people have a hard time participating in church life. People are busy in Hong Kong, and families demand a lot of young people. They don't want the young people to spend too much time at church. --Hong Kong Mennonite*

on the young from the drug culture and the difficulty of resisting a drive for material possessions.

We also observed important participation in the life of the church by young people. Throughout Africa, youth choirs are central to both the worship and outreach of local congregations. In Central America young people serve the church as volunteer community health workers and catechists. In India a movement of young people formed into groups to live among and learn from the poor.

> Eighty percent of our members are under 30, but we don't call what they do in church a "youth movement" because that is threatening to the government. -- Ethiopian church leader

Recently Raymond Fung, evangelism secretary of the WCC, commented in his newsletter that the crisis of evangelism among the young is one of the most pressing problems of the worldwide church. The crisis affects both extremely marginalized youth and those who live closer to the center of society and the church. Fung calls for a commitment to long-term incarnational mission among marginalized youth. He also questions all Christians, young and old, to find out what about the church will really draw young people into commitment. We believe this question and this call must be taken very seriously (Fung 1989:4-5).

D. Third World theologies

This quite inadequate label is used to speak both of formal efforts made by theologians from various parts of the world and informal expressions of Christians everywhere about the understandings of faith. There are well-known theologies with worldwide effect such as the liberation theologies. There are diverse movements with similar theological presuppositions, such as the independent church phenomenon in Africa and pentecostalism in Latin America. There are theological systems which develop in relationship to more specific context: *minjung* theology in Korea is a well-known example. We assume there are other such expressions which are so specific and immediate that they have not been named or become known to the broader Christian world.

> African Independent Churches are churches of the people, not institutions. People feel that the church is them, that the leadership is serving them. Once a church becomes an institution, it begins to lose many characteristics of the church of God. --staff person, Organization of African Independent Churches

There are at least two tendencies among western/northern or outside Christians towards such theologies. One is to be fascinated by them, to study them, and to make efforts to define the outside theological understandings in the same or similar terms. The other is to fear them, assuming that there is something inherently untrustworthy about their presuppositions and acting as if it is the outsiders' role to maintain theological orthodoxy.

The writers believe that mission and service workers should meet any theological expression in the new setting with respect and deep interest. Northerners/westerners must first be open to what they can learn from these theologies and then look for positive non-threatening opportunities to discuss them with the Christians working them out. The points we do not understand or agree with should not immediately be assumed to be wrong. Our primary energy should never go into arguing either against these points or the theology in general. Our challenge should always be to be working out, from our own faith, history and experience, the theological understandings which strengthen our common witness in that given place.

A missionary who wants to come to Latin America should keep in mind three worlds--liberation theology, the pentecostal-charismatic movement, and Roman Catholicism as a culture. Those not familiar with those worlds will be out of orbit. -- Argentine Baptist pastor

If we Mennonites had followed our principles, liberation theology should have been invented by us. Not the Marxist analysis, but the option for the poor and the desire to see things change. To say we do not agree and have the courage to accept the consequences. --Mexican Mennonite Bible professor

The government's religious policy is trying to set up a civil religion. The church, as a protege of the government, does not want to jeopardize its position by speaking out. I have tried without success to get the council of churches to set up a department of human rights. Of course we give alms to poor people. We do good things. But what do we say about this dictatorship? -- Indonesian Christian lawyer

E. Ideology

As conveyors of myths and symbols which move large groups of people, ideologies can be either interwoven with or confused with religions. Ideologies always challenge the understandings of Christians as well as other people of faith.

Ideologies seek to assert control over the lives of people. In some cases ideological systems take on political form when they attain power through force; these systems tend to enforce upon people compliance with the practices identifying the ideology. In other cases ideological systems attain credibility through resistance to some form of power or oppression; in such cases the systems tend to attract adherents among those disenfranchised by the power system.

Christian and other believers who ask questions about ideologies are often isolated and viewed with suspicion. Believers whose faith pushes them to know or even support ideological movements also lead difficult and lonely lives. North American mission and service workers in other parts of the world need to be ideologically aware and equipped for the discussion which arises when ideology confronts faith.

F. Ambivalence about institutions in the church

The history of the western church has been a highly institutional one, and in a corresponding way western/northern mission involvements elsewhere in the world have also lead to the emergence of institutional forms of church. Mission workers started schools so that new believers could learn to read the Bible. They developed compounds to provide shelter and community for new believers away from their home environments. They built clinics and hospitals to care for physical illnesses and injuries. In more recent times, when western/ northern agencies began to sense difficulties with institutional forms of mission-church, issues of constructing church buildings for new congregations and operating Bible schools to train church leaders persisted in demanding attention.

Young people who have gone through both the government's youth rites and confirmation into the church are asking more questions about what it means to be a Christian in this society. They have found that Marxist ideology is not enough. --East German professor

In our church institutions we have lost the movement of the Spirit. Schools and hospitals have been a witness, but they also cater to rich people. Institutions strive for more and more power, prestige and position. How can they be converted into symbols of the mind of Christ? --Church of South India bishop

It is not surprising that churches which grew up in the midst of western/northern mission efforts have defined themselves institutionally. In many places these institutional manifestations of church have gained great respect and gratitude from beyond as well as within the church. Institutions of the church have made contributions to many societies. At the same time institutions have both been a great burden to churches and led to very serious questions. In many places Christians wonder whether the church is able to sustain the weight of the institutions it is responsible for. They also ask whether anyone outside their own setting is willing to help them in bearing that weight. Others ask whether the institutions are still doing what the church in a given place should be doing.

If you have not been to a mission school you have not been to school. --Nigerian university lecturer

Church schools provide an excellent case in point. In many parts of the world these schools are reputed to provide the best education available, and everyone pushes to get their children into church schools. This competition inevitably turns schools into places of privilege. Others question whether the education offered in the formal school system really responds to the needs of their societies.

People from other parts of the world observe the western/northern church, note its high degree of institutionalization, and wonder why we are so unwilling to allow our resources to be used for institutional development in their settings. They wonder what changed our minds from the days when our agencies apparently poured resources into their communities for that purpose.

The writers believe that North American mission and service agencies need to join more freely in the international discussion about value of and support for church institutions both in our own communities and in other parts of the world. We believe it will be more necessary to be more open-handed on these questions in the days ahead. At the same time, we believe that the most vibrant future of the church is in less institutional forms, and that such a shift is cause for thanksgiving. Where a need for new church institutions becomes evident, we call on all Christians to renew the old mission urges to unite and cooperate in order to develop institutions which serve many rather than a few. We urge all the churches to be willing to take on a serious search for new forms, so that the move away from institutions will be liberating rather than seen as defeat.

VIII. Recommendations and specific suggestions

In this section the writers list general recommendations that we commend to Mennonite Church mission and service agencies for their considered action, as well as specific suggestions which we see following from those recommendations. Reference to "the agencies" includes all MC agencies. Other references designate individual or larger groups of agencies. The specific suggestions are referenced to applicable points in the text.

A. Increase mission personnel

More persons should be called to join the broad spectrum of mission tasks, from relief and development to evangelism to the witness for justice and peace. North American agencies should work out placements for all our personnel in consultation with churches and interchurch partners in other parts of the world. We assume international churches are also sending their own workers in mission and that North American personnel will usually work together with them in the various mission tasks of that setting. An important part of preparing for mission tasks is for personnel to go through learning and exchange experiences. These experiences should involve both more North Americans and more people from elsewhere, and should represent learning opportunities both north-south and south-south.

1. The agencies should re-conceive all short-term mission and service opportunities for North Americans to be primarily for the purpose of learning and exchange with Christians in other places. These learning-exchange experiences should be considered as important times for participants to consider and for agencies and host churches to recruit for long-term assignments (IV.E.2)

2. The agencies, with the invitation to all CIM agencies to join them, should appoint a staff person to coordinate existing--and develop

new--exchange programs internationally. Exchange opportunities should be expanded to include older persons, those representing different vocational groups, and those involved in specific areas of church work--evangelism, youth work, etc. (IV.B.1, IV.E.2).

3. The agencies should take steps to recruit and appoint more women, especially single women, for international assignments in leadership training, church liaison, evangelism and justice/ peace activities/presence (III.C,D,E, II.B).

4. The agencies, together with congregations and regional conferences, should begin to recruit and prepare a group of people available to work as nonresident mission relationship and training persons internationally. These persons would be available for a specific period of time each year to visit, encourage, and offer teaching or other requested resources, to host churches and interchurch groups, with the support of both the agency concerned and the sending congregation or conference. The latter would commit itself to provide employment for the periods of time when the person is in North America. The nonresident worker would need careful preparation in the history, culture and language of the country or region in which he/she would work, with the assumption that he/she would maintain long-term contact in one place rather than visit many different places. He/she might also be employed in North America to work in a related community to the culture being visited/served on a short-term non-resident basis (e.g., a teacher to India working among Indian or other students from the subcontinent in a North American setting). In some setting a nonresident worker with technical skills might be able to arrange short leaves from a North American professional establishment (III.D.3, IV.B.7).

5. The agencies should give new attention to the formal or informal role host churches and groups play in training North American workers, both during a short-term internship learning exchange assignment and for those who move into longer-term placements (IV.E.2,3).

6. Agencies should give attention to an in-service training plan for long-term workers as part of the discussion of their commitment to that service, including additional language training, study at a Mennonite college or seminary, study at a missiological training institution, and possible study in third-world theological training institutions (IV.E.4).

B. Give priority to equipping and preparing leaders

North American Mennonite agencies should gratefully accept the call from churches around the world, a call stating that North American mission workers can be most helpful to them by continuing, renewing and exploring a variety of leadership training options. North Americans must understand that accepting this priority means offering resources and being available for discussion rather than assuming that North American answers fit the leadership questions in other places. We must also understand that any sort of church leadership is assumed to be on behalf of people rather than an opportunity for increased power and privilege.

1. The agencies, with invitation to all CIM member agencies to join them, should set up an international or a series of regional scholarship funds for the training of church people in other parts of the world. Decisions about disbursement of the fund(s) and places of study would be made by an international or regional group representing churches in those places. The majority of scholarships should be for biblical, theological and ecclesiastical studies, but in certain cases preparation for other professional disciplines could also be supported (III.D.3.c).
2. The agencies, in discussion with their partner churches, should provide opportunities for those churches to train several members who could serve as translators regionally or internationally. Languages of need would be determined by the churches in a case-by-case discussion (III.D.3.c).
3. The agencies should recruit mission and service workers in leadership training assignments, agency administrators, and other international church workers to serve in a network with the task of seeking out and studying the variety of congregational and church leadership models in use around the world. This information should be widely disseminated among churches and be brought into all planning of new leadership training programs churches and agencies will implement (III.D.3).
4. Agencies should consider setting up new study centers and supporting those already in existence, both as witness and as training possibilities on behalf of the growth of churches in many international urban settings. Opportunities for interchurch cooperation in the development of study centers should be pursued (III.D.3.d).
5. Agencies should give high priority to the preparation and development of literature and audiovisual materials designed specifically for the use of churches in other parts of the world. This material should include both translated and adapted North American Mennonite material and material which is prepared locally/regionally. Contact with various interchurch centers which

train people in literature/AV development should be established to determine whether and how Mennonite agencies could support such efforts (III.D.3.d).

6. Agencies should organize an ad hoc study group in discussion with partner churches internationally to seek better understanding of the problems faced by new congregations in a variety of environments. The group should be given responsibility to find a deeper understanding of common issues which face many new congregations, to suggest specific steps by which these congregations can either be supported through such problems or if possible avoid them (III.D.2).

C. Decentralize structures

American Mennonite agencies should take steps to remove certain tasks from their decision-making spheres and give their support to the development of other church structures which can take up those tasks and make decisions about how they should be carried out. This process of decentralization is particularly important in financial areas; for real changes to take place in north/west-south/east church relationships, North American agencies must be willing to let others decide how to use some of the money which we have to contribute to tasks of mission worldwide. We must also be willing to be more open with partner churches about how much money is available to our agencies and how it is disbursed in general.

1. The agencies should initiate a series of regional interchurch conversations about whether, when and how they should contribute to the support of church workers in those parts of the world. Criteria for such support would need to be established, the following issues should be considered:

   a. Support for leadership training rather than for regular congregational or church administration positions.

   b. Support when a person faces enticement to work in the north/west or in the public sector because no positions with salary are available in the south/east or the church structure.

   c. Support where a church institution is heavily staffed by expatriates and seeks to increase indigenous presence in leadership.

   d. Support where the agency contributes expatriates and wants to express commitment to indigenous presence as well.

   e. Support where a person is working in a position which provides interchurch ministry rather than to only one congregation or denomination.

   f. Support where a regional church decision-making group approves.

g.   Support where local churches request outside help for a specific task which needs to be done but which they cannot do alone (V.B).

2.   The agencies should take active steps to designate a percentage of budgets to international or regional church funds over which we do not have decision-making power (see D below). As a specific way to provide money for some North American contributions to such funds, the agencies should set up projects which make direct links between North American church situations and those in other places. Specifically,

a.   Request that congregations, conferences and agencies place a voluntary two percent tax on all new building construction they undertake, to be contributed to a fund which would be used for costs of church and church-related building in other parts of the world.

b.   Request that all agency administrators, all church members who travel personally and all learning tour participants contribute one percent of their international travel costs, to be used for national and regional mission exchange travel in other parts of the world (V.B,C).

3.   MCC should take the lead in helping the agencies prepare a manual of experiences in church self-support projects internationally and in pursuing a study of new or alternative self-support options (V.D, VII.F).

4.   The agencies appoint persons to develop much more extensive programs for congregation-to-congregation exchange and joint mission efforts between North America and other parts of the world (V.E.1-5).

5.   The agencies should seek opportunities to discuss with groups of church partners what our total budget is and how it is disbursed (VI.C).

D. Focus on inter-Mennonite and other interchurch international mission efforts

North American Mennonite agencies should be ready to work cooperatively at all levels--among different Mennonite conferences in North America, with various Mennonite churches in specific regions of the world where we have relationships, and with Christians from other churches as well as Mennonites in parts of the world where we take up the various tasks of mission.

1.   The agencies, with invitation to all CIM members to join them, should take initiative to approach Mennonite World Conference in order to find ways to greatly strengthen the regional inter-Mennonite organizations that exist--and perhaps in some circumstances assist the emergence of new ones. We should share,

although not impose, the vision that these regional bodies become structures which would share decision-making responsibility for a spectrum of Mennonite mission-service work in their regions (V.F, VI.E).

2. The agencies should encourage all North American workers and administrators to continually be alert to the work and presence of other church groups in any program location around the world; they should encourage all related North American Mennonites to establish and maintain contact with representatives of these groups, and whenever possible to consider ways of working cooperatively; the agencies should encourage partner Mennonite churches to look to sister churches in a region as resources, to explore places where joint mission efforts might be undertaken by these different local groups. Under no circumstances should North American agencies discourage or stand in the way of efforts by partner churches to build contacts with other local church groups (V.F; VI.D,E; VII.F).

3. At least one-quarter of money available from North American Mennonite agencies for international exchange programs should be contributed for south/south church exchanges (V.C.6).

4. The agencies--with encouragement to other CIM members to join them--should organize a conference on mission in its various forms (relief and development, witness for justice and peace, evangelism, helping a church take form) among indigenous communities around the world. Members of indigenous communities whom we know, as well as Mennonite and other persons who have worked in indigenous communities, could serve as resource persons (III.H.3, VII.A).

IX. Reading list

The following reading list refers to books and periodicals the writers have been influenced by while working on the study project. The number of missiological, anthropological, ecclesiastical and other related works that have been published in the past few decades goes far beyond our capacity to record in this space.

Barrett, David B., ed.
  1982 *World Christian Encyclopedia*. Nairobi: Oxford University Press.
  1989 "Tracking Megatrends in Mission," in *World Evangelization*. 16, 59:28-32.
Beeson, Trevor
  1982 *Discretion and Valour*. Philadelphia: Fortress Press.
Blauw, Johannes
  1962 *The Missionary Nature of the Church: A Survey of the Biblical Theology of Mission*. Grand Rapids, MI: William B. Eerdmans Publishing Company.
Bonk, Jon
  1986 "The Role of Affluence in the Christian Missionary Enterprise from the West," in *Missiology*. XIV, 4:437-461.
Buhlmann, Walbert
  1986 *The Church of the Future: A Model for the Year 2001*. Maryknoll, NY: Orbis Books.
Burger, Julian
  1987 *Report from the Frontier: The State of the World's Indigenous Peoples*. London: Zed Books.
Cosmao, Vincent
  1984 *Changing the World: An Agenda for the Churches*. Maryknoll, NY: Orbis Books.

Costas, Orlando E.
1982   *Christ Outside the Gate: Mission Beyond Christendom*. Maryknoll, NY: Orbis Books.

Das, Somen, ed.
1987   *Christian Faith and Multiform Culture in India*. Bangalore: United Theological College.

Ela, Jean-Marc
1986   *African Cry*. Maryknoll, NY: Orbis Books.

Escobar, Samuel and Driver, John
1978   *Christian Mission and Social Justice*. Scottdale, PA: Herald Press.

Fung, Raymond
1989   "A Monthly Letter on Evangelism." 3/4:4,5.
        All issues of this letter have been extremely provocative and helpful to the writers.

Hesselgrave, David J.
1988   *Today's Choices for Tomorrow's Mission: An Evangelical Perspective on Trends and Issues in Missions*. Grand Rapids, MI: Zondervan Publishing House.

Hiebert, Paul G.
1985   *Anthropological Insights for Missionaries*. Grand Rapids, MI: Baker Book House.

Horner, Norman A.
1989   *A Guide to Christian Churches in the Middle East*. Elkhart, IN: Mission Focus Publications.

International Urban Associates
1989   "The Biblical Values and Principles Guiding International Urban Associates," in *IUA Newsletter*, Chicago, IL. I, 1:4.

Johnstone, Patrick
1986   *Operation World*. Waynesboro, GA: STL Books.

Kisare, Z. Marwa
1984   *Kisare: A Mennonite of Kiseru, An Autobiography as told to Joseph C. Shenk*. Salunga, PA: Eastern Mennonite Board of Missions and Charities.

Koyama, Kosuke
1984   *Mount Fuji and Mount Sinai: A Critique of Idols*. Maryknoll, NY: Orbis Books.

Loewen, Jacob A.
1975   *Culture and Human Values: Christian Intervention in Anthropological Perspective*. Pasadena, CA: William Carey Library.

Mar Gregorios, Paulos
1988   *The Meaning and Nature of Diakonia*. Geneva: WCC Publications.

Marchant, Colin
1985   *Signs in the City*. London: Hodder & Stoughton.

Metzler, James E.

1985   *From Saigon to Shalom: The Pilgrimage of a Missionary in Search of a More Authentic Mission.* Scottdale, PA: Herald Press.

Mission Focus

1988   Eight articles from a Consultation on Missiological Issues Facing the Church in Century 21 held at Mennonite Brethren Biblical Seminary. Vol. 16, No. 4:65-100.

Newbigin, Lesslie

1984   *The Other Side of 1984.* Geneva: WCC Publications.

1986   *Foolishness to the Greeks: The Gospel and Western Culture.* Grand Rapids, MI: William B. Eerdmans Publishing Company.

1987   *Mission in Christ's Way.* Geneva: WCC Publications.

Padilla, Rene C.

1985   *Mission Between the Times.* Grand Rapids, MI: William B. Eerdmans Publishing House.

Ramseyer, Robert L., ed.

1979   *Mission and the Peace Witness: The Gospel and Christian Discipleship.* Scottdale, PA: Herald Press.

Shenk, Wilbert R.

1988   *God's New Economy: Interdependence and Mission.* Elkhart, IN: Mission Focus Publications.

Shenk, Wilbert R., ed.

1980   *Mission Focus: Current Issues.* Scottdale, PA: Herald Press.

1984   *Anabaptism and Mission.* Scottdale, PA: Herald Press.

Stewart, Edward C.

1972   *American Cultural Patterns: A Cross-Cultural Perspective.* Yarmouth, ME: Intercultural Press.

Stott, John, ed.

1982   *Evangelism and Social Responsibility: An Evangelical Commitment.* Lausanne Committee for World Evangelization and the World Evangelical Fellowship.

Wilson, Samuel and Siewert, John, ed.

1986   *Mission Handbook.* Monrovia, CA: Missions Advanced Research and Communication Center.

World Council of Churches

1982   "Mission and Evangelism--An Ecumenical Affirmation," in *International Review of Mission.* LXXI, 284:427-451.

Proposal
Mennonite International Study Project

NANCY HEISEY/PAUL LONGACRE

Background

Included in the Goals for 1995 adopted by the Mennonite General Assembly was one defining the direction of the church in international mission and service: "to increase the number of workers supported in mission beyond North America from about 500 to 1,000." Following the assembly, representatives of five agencies--EMBMC, Franconia Conference International Mission Committee, MBM, MCC, and Virginia Conference Mission Board--met to determine ways in which they might respond. A consensus reached was that in order to better determine the nature of future Mennonite mission/service involvement it was important to study the world situation in search of fresh approaches for Christian ministry and to engage in dialogue with counterparts in other countries on their perceptions of the North American role in the ongoing work and witness of the church. After further discussion, Paul Longacre and Nancy Heisey accepted the assignment "to arrange settings where we can listen to Christians in other countries and cultures communicate their vision for evangelism, outreach, and Christian service in order to discover what role North American Christians should play in the worldwide community of faith, and bring back suggestions of creative methods through which we can participate with them in extending God's rule in the world."

Methodology

1. We propose to spend 50 percent of a two-year period from July 1987 to June 1989 traveling in five regions: Europe, Asia, Latin America, Africa and the Middle East. We hope to meet people in:
   a. church, interchurch and parachurch agency offices
   b. retreat and conference centers
   c. congregations and congregational (e.g., women's) groups
   d. home and social contacts
   e. "on the road"

2. While being dependent upon Mennonite mission and service personnel for many contacts and keeping them informed of our activities, we hope wherever possible of travel by locally available means, stay in church-related accommodations and use resources of translators who are from the area being visited.

3. The schedule attempts to reflect walking in the tension between visiting all the important places and spending long enough in any one

place to gain some real understanding. It is our hope that in many cases more than one conversation with those contacted will be possible.

4. During travel we hope to schedule rest/reflection days in order to be able to assimilate the weight of input received.

5. In North America we hope to establish and maintain contact with:
a. the supporting agencies
b. other Mennonite mission agencies
c. Council of International Ministries
d. Mennonite World Conference
e. North American individuals with mission experience/expertise
f. international Christians visiting/studying in North America.

6. It is a goal to stay up-to-date in mission/development/service literature, both periodicals and books. A bibliography is being established for which recommendations are welcome.

7. A reference group composed of appointees from each sponsoring agency will be formed as early as possible in the process, with whom meetings/conversations will be arranged in connection with the several stages of travel and reporting during the period.

Themes/Issues

The group of issues listed below outline the criteria by which initial identification of places to be visited were made:

I.   Religious environments
    A.   World religions: Islam, Hinduism, Buddhism
    B.   "Catholic" churches: Roman Catholic, Orthodox, Ancient
    C.   Post-Christian environments
        1.   Marxist/post-Marxist
        2.   secular
    D.   Traditional religions

II. Issues of specific relevance to Mennonites
    A.   areas of openness to western involvement
    B.   areas of serious restriction to western presence
    C.   older Mennonite mission areas
    D.   newer Mennonite mission areas
    E.   areas with no Mennonite involvement
    F.   areas with less frequent contact/less expertise within the North American Mennonite world

III. Groups to contact (in addition to/within the context of religious environments noted in I above)
    A.   Mennonite and Brethren in Christ churches
    B.   National and regional Christian councils
    C.   Pentecostal/faith mission churches
    D.   Independent churches/new religious movements
    E.   Evangelical fellowships
    F.   Peace/human rights groups

G. "Church leaders' children"--2nd and 3rd generation Christians and post-Christians in non-western settings

IV. Sociopolitical environments
   A. war/conflict zones
   B. military governments/national security states
   C. progressive revolutionary environments
   D. western or eastern satellites
   E. different economic situations: poor/developing/industrialized
   F. rural and urban settings

Tentative travel plans

I. Europe: September 27-December 5, 1987
   London--4 days
   Birmington--7 days
   France--5 days
   Spain--6 days
   Sicily/Italy--6 days/rest
   Netherlands--4 days
   W. Germany--4 days
   E. Germany--7 days
   Yugoslavia--4 days
   Cyprus--4 days/rest
   Egypt--10 days

II. Asia: January 15-April 30, 1988
   Geneva--7 days
   Kuwait--5 days
   India--21 days/rest
   Bangkok--5 days
   Burma--7 days
   Indonesia--14 days
   Singapore--5 days/rest
   Philippines--5 days
   Hong Kong--5 days
   South Korea--7 days
   Japan--14 days

III. Latin America: September-early December 1988
   Guatemala (one month for Nancy, including Spanish language study); during same period Paul would visit Trinidad and/or Jamaica)
   El Salvador
   Venezuela
   French Guyana
   Bolivia
   Uruguay

Argentina
Chile
Brazil
Mexico
Cuba
IV. Africa: January-April 1989
Cote d'Ivoire
Burkina Faso
Ghana
Benin
Zaire
South Africa
Botswana
Swaziland/Mozambique
Tanzania
Kenya (Nairobi)
Somalia
Sudan
West Bank/Israel

A final visit to Europe for reporting to European Mennonite mission groups may also be scheduled.

Reporting

Written reports on contacts and observations in each region will be prepared. A final report including observations, possibilities and suggestions will also be made. These reports will be shared with administrators, the reference committee and representatives of the churches visited.

Further discussion is in order on other "end products" which might grow out of this assignment for use in North American churches.

Proposed Budget 1987-1989
Mennonite International Study Project

Item:	1987	1988	1989	Total
Salary/benefits	$17,750	$35,500	$17,750	$71,000
International travel	5,000	14,500	8,000	27,500
Local travel/expenses	3,800	7,400	3,800	15,000
Reference group	1,750	2,000	1,750	5,500
Office/secretarial	4,000	7,500	4,000	15,500
Books	200	300	0	500
Total	$32,500	$67,200	$35,300	$135,000

July 1987

Mennonite International Study Project

The Mennonite International Study Project is sponsored by mission and service agencies of the Mennonite Church in North America. The purpose of the study project is: "1) to arrange settings where North Americans can listen to Christians in other countries and cultures as they communicate their vision for evangelism, outreach and Christian service, in order to discover what role North American Christians should play in the worldwide community of faith, and 2) to bring back suggestions of creative methods through which we can participate with Christians in other parts of the world in extending God's rule in the world."

Paul Longacre and Nancy Heisey are a married couple who have been assigned by the Mennonite Church to carry out this study project over a two-year period from 1987 to 1989. They have traveled for six months in Europe, the Middle East and Asia and are planning trips to Latin America and Africa in order to meet church and interchurch groups and individual Christians in these places. Some specific questions Paul and Nancy ask of those they meet are:

1. How do you describe your role as Christians in your society? What kinds of mission and service work are Christians in your region or country involved in?

2. What are some visions you have about mission and service work that you would like to do?

3. (For those in the Mennonite "family"): What is the meaning of your Mennonite identity in your witness?

4. What are ways that Christians from North America have worked in your country? What parts of their work have you found helpful or not helpful? What new ways can you propose for working together at mission and service tasks with North American Christians?

Paul and Nancy would like to meet with many different people: church leaders and lay people; women as well as men; young and older people, city and rural dwellers. They hope to have many conversations and social contacts as well as formal meetings and interviews. They want to worship and pray with the churches in places they visit.

Paul previously worked for Mennonite Central Committee in Vietnam and Indonesia, and later as administrator for MCC's programs throughout Asia. He also served as member of the Overseas Committee of Mennonite Board of Missions. Nancy worked with MCC in Zaire and then as administrator for MCC's Africa program. Together Paul and Nancy served as MCC country representatives in Burkina Faso.

June 1988

XI. A statement of response and commitment by the sponsoring program agencies

Preamble

As the twentieth century draws to a close, we give thanks to God and commend the faithful witnesses of the past for helping to establish the Church of Jesus Christ on every continent. With the dawning of the twenty-first century, we rejoice in exciting new opportunities to cooperate with the worldwide family of brothers and sisters in mission to people who have not heard the good news, have not chosen to come to faith in Christ, or have not felt at ease participating in the church. The energetic spirit and the gifts of Christians in both new and historic Christian communities around the world bring fresh dimensions to the task of mission. They are asking North Americans to join with them and to offer them our resources as together we are renewed and empowered for the work of the kingdom in the decades ahead. The challenge is to see the global church focus its resources on the mission task worldwide.

Nature of Mission

Mission originates in the nature and purpose of God. The missio Dei pervades all of history as God calls out a people who will be the instrument of "blessing" for all peoples by dispersing them throughout the world. The people of God are called to bear witness by word and deed to all that God has done in Jesus Christ for the "healing of the nations." The people of God participate in God's mission under the power and direction of the Holy Spirit. The treasure of the gospel is carried in "earthen" vessels. At times the vessels obscure the treasure. Thus we must continually submit our efforts to the judging and purifying actions of the Holy Spirit if they are to serve the missio Dei.

Human Transformation

There is only one gospel, one source of human transformation. Both evangelism and development must draw on that source which is found in the work of God in Jesus Christ. Biblical anthropology does not separate the human being into spiritual and physical. Such dualistic thinking is a preoccupation of western Christians. The universal human predicament is that sin is present in every human being and has resulted in alienation of each individual from God and other human beings. This affects all aspects of life: physical, spiritual, psychological, and social. For this condition God provides an answer. The biblical mandate calls the people of God to evangelize--that is to invite women and men to surrender themselves to Jesus Christ and follow God's will in all of life--and compassionately demonstrate God's way of peace, justice, human well-being and respect for God's creation in practical and concrete action.

The Role of the Congregation

World mission is integral to the nature of the church. Evangelism done in the way of Jesus will result in making disciples who will form communities of worship, fellowship, and mission. Each congregation becomes a basic building block and center for world mission. The local congregation has a special role in preparing and training leaders with a vision for the world. The congregation's life and ministries should be structured to help members experience and participate in extending the rule of God around the world. Mission agencies can facilitate and network these local congregations for the tasks of world mission, but mission agencies are supporting structures enabling congregations to call, train, and send forth workers. Teams of trained workers will reproduce themselves and form vital, caring, witnessing congregations in yet other communities around the world. World mission today should be seen as the multilateral cooperation and partnership of thousands of congregations of God's people working together, exchanging and coordinating God-given gifts and resources, joyfully inviting all people to share salvation and life under the lordship of Jesus Christ.

Exchanges

The pattern of Christian mission has frequently been one way, perceived as flowing from the resource rich to the resource poor. We praise God that that era is ending. Whatever the mistakes of the past, the church now encircles the globe. We in the North have been slow to understand that our brothers and sisters from around the world can enrich us and enrich each other. In order to realize that vision, we as North American church agencies will commit more resources: a) to enable churches in the two-thirds world to send their representatives into our midst to minister to us and to share their gifts with us; b) to

72

enable exchanges between churches of two-thirds world countries so that these churches can learn from each other and minister to each other in a spirit of mutual respect and equality. This sharing of resources will be done in a spirit of trust and openness and may include providing funds bilaterally to churches so that they can implement such exchanges. It may also mean providing resources to regional church structures so that they can cooperatively determine how best to implement exchanges.

Partnership and Decentralization of Power

The church has become a global community with congregations present in every nation/state on earth. The Anabaptist family of churches has participated in this growth of the church; our family now worships in about 110 languages every Sunday. The presence and diversity of the church worldwide is the most significant asset as the church considers mission and service.

When North Americans are involved in cross-cultural evangelism or development work, those commitments should always take place in counsel and, where possible, in partnership with other disciples of Jesus. When North American Mennonites are involved in mission and service, it will be as participants in cross-cultural teams, often under the authority and the mandate of the overseas Mennonite churches.

Ways must be devised for our overseas partners to speak to the manner in which our priorities are developed and the funds and personnel shared. Some circumstances will require a shift from bilateral relationships to multilateral regional consultation. Mission and service agencies should share resources and participate in decentralizing decision-making so that all partners can exercise their calling to witness and serve.

Women and Marginalized in Ministry

The gospel message breaks walls of separation. It stands over and beyond class, gender, nationality, race, or occupation. Therefore, followers of Jesus Christ will embody respect for all people as images of God. This is especially true for those who are dehumanized and marginalized by majority social systems and powers. Women worldwide continue to be pioneers in evangelism. Sisters are the faithful core in many congregations. Mission agencies need to give high priority to making resources available to women, including income-earning possibilities, literacy training, family life education, and reading materials. Believing women will continue to provide long-term, low-profile leadership in the task of world evangelism.

Leadership Training

We acknowledge the urgent need for training leaders in the growing number of congregations and church structures overseas. We believe careful study should be made of unmet needs, effective programs, and possible cooperative ventures in leadership training. We recognize that western leadership models can be inappropriate in other cultures and commit ourselves to join partners in the search for models that meet the needs in their settings. We affirm that leadership training should be in the context of local churches such as institutes and seminars, and regional upper level Anabaptist leadership training such as SEMILLA in Central America. We wish to assist by developing trainers and by providing scholarships as requested by the local church, primarily for biblical, theological, mission and ecclesiastical studies.

Urbanization

This century has become the era of the city. The twentieth century, begun with 230 million urban people, will conclude with over 3 billion city dwellers. The cities of our world are nurturing a universal urban culture which is technological and communications-based. The cities affect entire regions and the global community with their cultural diffusion and linkages with kinship groups throughout the hinterland and, in many circumstances, other regions of the world.

The church in faithful mission and service must be present within the city. Evangelism, church formation, social action and justice making need to be combined in holistic ministry within the urban centers of our world. One approach to reaching unevangelized people groups with the gospel is to focus on the city where people are often more open to change and where those who come to faith in Christ may be able to share the Good News with their kinfolk elsewhere.

Short-Term/Long-Term Service

The call to mission is the call to serve. Quality of commitment and self-giving involvement have been and will continue to be the primary characteristics of cross-cultural mission.

The presence of the church calls for new levels of mutual regard in the placement of people. Sensitivity to an invitation, a concern for strengthening local congregations and the possibility of exchanges can help overcome the tendency to unidirectional thinking. Short-term assignments (up to two years) are valuable for specific assignments or educational preparation. Longer-term assignments call for solid language training and theological understanding for dealing with varied cultural contexts.

Christian Unity

Jesus prayed that the church be one for effectiveness in witness to the world. We affirm that there is only one Lord, one faith, one baptism, and one body of Christ. We are called to make that unity visible so that the world may believe. But we are often hindered by our humanity, as were the Corinthians whom Paul called carnal. Our limited knowledge, our particular historical experience, our different understandings and theological preferences can impede the full expression of the unity God intends. God calls us to experience the grace of unity in Christ and thereby overcome the divisiveness of human sinfulness and the sociological forces of in-group insularity.

As Mennonites, we offer our particular history and our theological heritage as a gift to be shared with the whole body of Christ while receiving from other Christian families their unique gifts. We see ourselves as a committed disciple group participating in the whole body of those who confess and follow Jesus as Lord without thereby denying our unique contribution nor negating the unity of the whole.

Call to Prayer

Prayer for each other is one of the most important mission tasks and the request most often repeated by churches overseas to Christians in North America. Prayer is one of the most significant gifts Christians offer to the world. At times it is the only gift we can offer. The act of praying for each other helps us experience the reality that both we in churches that are materially rich and those around the world who are part of materially poor churches are wholly dependent on God. It best exemplifies that we need each other to be engaged in mission.

A meeting of the five sponsoring agencies was held December 11, 1989, to receive and review the Final Report. The foregoing statement was drafted as a response.